or

a N. Russikoff, M.A.

tor in Chief

Massler Levin, M.A.

reative Director

aren J. Goldfluss, M.S. Ed.

llustrator

Clint McKnight

Cover Artist

Brenda DiAntonis

Art Coordinator

Renée Mc Elwee

Imaging

James Edward Grace

Craig Gunnell

Publisher

Mary D. Smith, M.S. Ed.

MATH STRATEGIES
to use with your
English Language
Learners

Teacher Created Resources

TCR 2910

Grades 5-6

Contains Standards and Benchmarks

...ssons
...lish speakers
...hers and students

Teacher Created Resources

Author

Tracie I. Heskett, M. Ed.

Teacher Created Resources

6421 Industry Way
Westminster, CA 92683
www.teachercreated.com

ISBN: 978-1-4206-2910-1

© 2012 Teacher Created Resources
Made in U.S.A.

Teacher Created Resources

Table of Contents

Table of Contents *(cont.)*

Introduction

Teachers across the country are experiencing increasing numbers of English language learners (ELLs) in their regular education classrooms. As ELL student populations grow, teachers need strategies to reach these students. Many lessons in existing curricula are designed for native speakers of English and are not tailored to support second language acquisition. The lessons and strategies in this book accommodate the needs of ELLs.

Math Strategies to Use With Your English Language Learners offers teachers ways to teach specific math concepts and skills to ELLs and at-risk students in regular education classrooms. This book includes math teaching strategies and skills, two glossaries of common math terms and verbs, and sample lessons and activities. The purpose of this book is to help teachers make math lessons comprehensible to their ELL students.

The following are a few of the most frequently asked questions regarding ELL math instruction. The answers provided are general; for more specific answers, review the strategies in this book.

How do specific strategies help ELL students develop math skills?

Instructional strategies that focus on math and language skills support ELLs as they build English proficiency. Support in students' first language skills helps students develop their understanding of math concepts in English. Effective teaching strategies engage students and increase their motivation to learn.

Why is it that some ELLs are able to give answers to questions, but they can't explain how they arrived at the conclusions?

Various cultures approach math processes in different ways. The focus may be on arriving at the correct answer, rather than the steps students take to find the answer. In these cases, teachers will need to teach students how to explain their thought processes and answers.

How can I use interactive whiteboard technology to help my ELLs?

Interactive whiteboard technology can be an invaluable resource when working with ELLs. ELL instruction is often visually oriented; pictures, graphics, and other visual information help to increase student comprehension. Use interactive whiteboard technology to enhance the following:

- ✪ add variety to visual aids and graphic organizers.
- ✪ provide sentence frames for different language levels.
- ✪ help students mark text.
- ✪ display charts and tables.
- ✪ help students make connections between written and oral text.

How to Use This Book

The first section, *English Language Learner Instruction*, contains information on recognizing learning styles and establishing cultural connections. It also includes specific math skills that your students can learn and use independently. Tips for how to use instructional tools, such as manipulatives and technology, are also provided in this section. Additionally, this section addresses specific strategies teachers can use with their ELLs. A few of the strategies detailed are Case Studies, Math Journals, and Reciprocal Teaching. Each strategy page includes an explanation, examples, tips for teaching, and at least one sample activity.

The second section, *Math Language Connections*, contains vocabulary tips and activities, acknowledging that students need to understand math vocabulary in order to succeed in math. Also included are two glossaries—one of math terms and the other of math verbs. These glossaries are student-friendly, in that they contain definitions written in a simplified way (some definitions even have accompanying pictures). While you can use these glossaries as your own instructional tool, you may also wish to copy them for your students so they have a math resource to consult. A chart on confusing language patterns will help teachers understand some of the language obstacles ELLs face, as well as how to help students overcome them. This section concludes with a thorough review of how to help students "crack the code" of word problems.

The third section, *Practical Classroom Applications*, is composed of sample lessons and information on assessment and rubrics. Lessons include vocabulary and materials lists, as well as activity directions, handouts, and extensions. The resources, activities, and lessons provided will help you to incorporate ELL teaching strategies into math lessons.

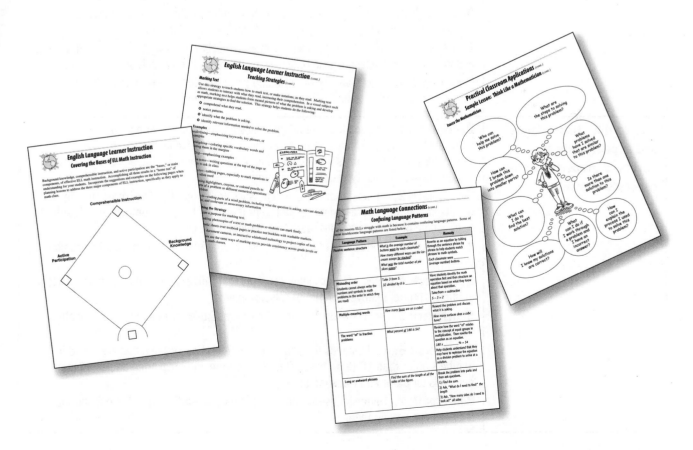

Standards and Benchmarks

Each activity in *Math Strategies to Use With Your English Language Learners* meets at least one of the following standards and benchmarks, which are used with permission from McREL. Copyright 2012 McREL. Mid-continent Research for Education and Learning, 4601 DTC Boulevard, Suite 500, Denver, Colorado 80237. Telephone: 303-337-0990. Website: *www.mcrel.org/standards-benchmarks*. To align McREL Standards to the Common Core Standards, go to *www.mcrel.org*.

Standards	Benchmarks
Standard 1. Uses a variety of strategies in the problem solving process	**Benchmark 1.** Understands how to break a complex problem into simpler parts or use a similar problem type to solve a problem **Benchmark 2.** Uses a variety of strategies to understand problem-solving situations and processes (e.g., considers different strategies and approaches to a problem, restates problem from various perspectives) **Benchmark 3.** Understands that there is no one right way to solve mathematical problems but that different methods (e.g., working backward from a solution, using a similar problem type, identifying a pattern) have different advantages and disadvantages **Benchmark 4.** Formulates a problem, determines information required to solve the problem, chooses methods for obtaining this information, and sets limits for acceptable solutions **Benchmark 5.** Represents problem situations in and translates among oral, written, concrete, pictorial, and graphical forms **Benchmark 6.** Generalizes from a pattern of observations made in particular cases, makes conjectures, and provides supporting arguments for these conjectures (i.e., uses inductive reasoning) **Benchmark 7.** Constructs informal logical arguments to justify reasoning process and methods of solutions to problems (i.e., uses informal deductive methods) **Benchmark 8.** Understands the role of written symbols in representing mathematical ideas and the use of precise language in conjunction with the special symbols of mathematics **Benchmark 9.** Uses a variety of reasoning processes (e.g., reasoning from a counter example, using proportionality) to model and to solve problems
Standard 2. Understands and applies basic and advanced properties of the concepts of numbers	**Benchmark 1.** Understands the relationships among equivalent number representations (e.g., whole numbers, positive and negative integers, fractions, ratios, decimals, percents, scientific notation, exponentials) and the advantages and disadvantages of each type of representation **Benchmark 2.** Understands the characteristics and properties (e.g., order relations, relative magnitude, base-ten place values) of the set of rational numbers and its subsets (e.g., whole numbers, fractions, decimals, integers) **Benchmark 3.** Understands the role of positive and negative integers in the number system **Benchmark 4.** Uses number theory concepts (e.g., divisibility and remainders, factors, multiples, prime, relatively prime) to solve problems **Benchmark 5.** Understands the characteristics and uses of exponents and scientific notation **Benchmark 6.** Understands the structure of numeration systems that are based in numbers other than 10 (e.g., base 60 for telling time and measuring angles, Roman numerals for dates and clock faces) **Benchmark 7.** Understands the concepts of ratio, proportion, and percent and the relationships among them

Standards and Benchmarks *(cont.)*

Standards	Benchmarks
Standard 3. Uses basic and advanced procedures while performing the processes of computation	**Benchmark 1.** Adds, subtracts, multiplies, and divides integers and rational numbers **Benchmark 2.** Adds and subtracts fractions with unlike denominators; multiplies and divides fractions **Benchmark 3.** Understands exponentiation of rational numbers and root-extraction (e.g., squares and square roots, cubes and cube roots) **Benchmark 4.** Selects and uses appropriate computational methods (e.g., mental, paper and pencil, calculator, computer) for a given situation **Benchmark 5.** Understands the correct order of operations for performing arithmetic computations **Benchmark 6.** Uses proportional reasoning to solve mathematical and real-world problems (e.g., involving equivalent fractions, equal ratios, constant rate of change, proportions, percents) **Benchmark 7.** Understands the properties of operations with rational numbers (e.g., distributive property, commutative and associative properties of addition and multiplication, inverse properties, identity properties) **Benchmark 8.** Knows when an estimate is more appropriate than an exact answer for a variety of problem situations **Benchmark 9.** Understands how different algorithms work for arithmetic computations and operations
Standard 4. Understands and applies basic and advanced properties of the concepts of measurement	**Benchmark 1.** Understands the basic concept of rate as a measure (e.g., miles per gallon) **Benchmark 2.** Solves problems involving perimeter (circumference) and area of various shapes (e.g., parallelograms, triangles, circles) **Benchmark 3.** Understands the relationships among linear dimensions, area, and volume and the corresponding uses of units, square units, and cubic units of measure **Benchmark 4.** Solves problems involving units of measurement and converts answers to a larger or smaller unit within the same system (i.e., standard or metric) **Benchmark 5.** Understands the concepts of precision and significant digits as they relate to measurement (e.g., how units indicate precision) **Benchmark 6.** Selects and uses appropriate units and tools, depending on degree of accuracy required, to find measurements for real-world problems **Benchmark 7.** Understands formulas for finding measures (e.g., area, volume, surface area) **Benchmark 8.** Selects and uses appropriate estimation techniques (e.g., overestimate, underestimate, range of estimates) to solve real-world problems **Benchmark 9.** Understands procedures for basic indirect measurements (e.g., using grids to estimate area of irregular figures)

Standards and Benchmarks *(cont.)*

Standards	Benchmarks
Standard 5. Understands and applies basic and advanced properties of the concepts of geometry	**Benchmark 1.** Uses geometric methods (i.e., an unmarked straightedge and a compass using an algorithm) to complete basic geometric constructions (e.g., perpendicular bisector of a line segment, angle bisector) **Benchmark 2.** Understands the defining properties of three-dimensional figures (e.g., a cube has edges with equal lengths, faces with equal areas and congruent shapes, right angle corners) **Benchmark 3.** Understands the defining properties of triangles (e.g., the sum of the measures of two sides of a triangle must be greater than the measure of the third side) **Benchmark 4.** Understands geometric transformations of figures (e.g., rotations, translations, dilations) **Benchmark 5.** Understands the relationships between two- and three-dimensional representations of a figure (e.g., scale drawings, blueprints, planar cross sections) **Benchmark 6.** Understands the mathematical concepts of similarity (e.g., scale, proportion, growth rates) and congruency **Benchmark 7.** Understands the basic concept of the Pythagorean theorem
Standard 6. Understands and applies basic and advanced concepts of statistics and data analysis	**Benchmark 1.** Understands basic characteristics of measures of central tendency (i.e., mean, mode, median) **Benchmark 2.** Understands basic characteristics of frequency and distribution (e.g., range, varying rates of change, gaps, clusters) **Benchmark 3.** Understands the basic concepts of center and dispersion of data **Benchmark 4.** Reads and interprets data in charts, tables, and plots (e.g., stem-and-leaf, box-and-whiskers, scatter) **Benchmark 5.** Uses data and statistical measures for a variety of purposes (e.g., formulating hypotheses, making predictions, testing conjectures) **Benchmark 6.** Organizes and displays data using tables, graphs (e.g., line, circle, bar), frequency distributions, and plots (e.g., stem-and-leaf, box-and-whiskers, scatter) **Benchmark 7.** Understands faulty arguments, common errors, and misleading presentation of data **Benchmark 8.** Understands that the same set of data can be represented using a variety of tables, graphs, and symbols and that different modes of representation often convey different messages (e.g., variation in scale can alter a visual message) **Benchmark 9.** Understands the basic concept of outliers **Benchmark 10.** Understands basic concepts about how samples are chosen (e.g., random samples, bias in sampling procedures, limited samples, sampling error)

Standards and Benchmarks *(cont.)*

Standards	Benchmarks
Standard 7. Understands and applies basic and advanced concepts of probability	**Benchmark 1.** Determines probability using mathematical/theoretical models (e.g., table or tree diagram, area model, list, sample space) **Benchmark 2.** Determines probability using simulations or experiments **Benchmark 3.** Understands how predictions are based on data and probabilities (e.g., the difference between predictions based on theoretical probability and experimental probability) **Benchmark 4.** Understands that the measure of certainty in a given situation depends on a number of factors (e.g., amount of data collected, what is known about the situation, how current data are) **Benchmark 5.** Understands the relationship between the numerical expression of a probability (e.g., fraction, percentage, odds) and the events that produce these numbers
Standard 8. Understands and applies basic and advanced properties of functions and algebra	**Benchmark 1.** Knows that an expression is a mathematical statement using numbers and symbols to represent relationships and real-world situations (e.g., equations and inequalities with or without variables) **Benchmark 2.** Understands that a variable can be used in many ways (e.g., as a placeholder for a specific unknown, such as $x + 8 = 13$; as a representative of a range of values, such as $4x + 7$) **Benchmark 3.** Understands various representations (e.g., tables, graphs, verbal descriptions, algebraic expressions, Venn diagram) of patterns and functions and the relationships among them **Benchmark 4.** Understands the basic concept of a function (i.e., functions describe how changes in one quantity or variable result in changes in another) **Benchmark 5.** Solves linear equations using concrete, informal, and formal methods (e.g., using properties, graphing ordered pairs, using slope-intercept form) **Benchmark 6.** Solves simple inequalities and non-linear equations with rational number solutions, using concrete and informal methods **Benchmark 7.** Understands spatial values (e.g., minimum and maximum values, x- and y-intercepts, slope, constant ratio or difference) of patterns, relationships, and functions **Benchmark 8.** Understands basic operations (e.g., combining like terms, expanding, substituting for unknowns) on algebraic expressions **Benchmark 9.** Uses the rectangular coordinate system to model and to solve problems **Benchmark 10.** Solves simple systems of equations graphically **Benchmark 11.** Understands the properties of arithmetic and geometric sequences (i.e., linear and exponential patterns)
Standard 9. Understands the general nature and uses of mathematics	**Benchmark 1.** Understands that mathematics has been helpful in practical ways for many centuries **Benchmark 2.** Understands that mathematicians often represent real things using abstract ideas like numbers or lines; they then work with these abstractions to learn about the things they represent

ESL Terms

The following are some of the most common terms used in ESL instruction. These terms are used throughout this book. For definitions of specific skills or strategies (e.g., clarifying, advance organizers, think-pair-share), look on pages 23–31 and 38–62.

Academic language: language used in the school environment, including words, phrases, grammar, and language structure, as well as academic terms and technical language

BICS: Basic Interpersonal Communication Skills; social, conversational language used with family and friends

Bilingual: speaking two languages fluently

CALP: Cognitive Academic Language Proficiency; formal language used in classrooms and with texts

Chunks/Chunking: information divided into units in order to be more comprehensible

Decoding: skills used (such as transfer) to decipher given information into understandable information

Differentiated instruction: modified instruction so that students of different abilities, knowledge, and skills can equally experience materials (e.g., providing multiple assignments within a teaching unit that are tailored for students with differing language levels)

EFL: English as a Foreign Language

ELL: English Language Learner

ESL: English as a Second Language

Explicit instruction: otherwise known as "direct instruction"; learners are provided with specific information or directions about what is to be learned.

Fluency: ability to read, write, and speak a language easily, naturally, and accurately

Language acquisition: the natural process of learning a language; second language acquisition usually includes formal study

Language proficiency: ability to communicate and understand oral (listening and speaking) and written (reading and writing) academic and nonacademic language

Multicultural: relating to multiple cultural groups

Native language: first language learned and spoken

Native speakers of English (or native English speakers): individuals whose first language is English

Realia: real objects used for tactile demonstrations and for improving students' understanding (e.g., bringing in household examples of three-dimensional items in the shapes of cubes, pyramids, spheres, etc.)

Transfer (as in language transfer): applying knowledge and skills from a first language to a second language

Wait time: amount of time that elapses between a question or instruction and the next verbal response

ESL Objectives

Standards-based instruction aligns lessons with standards that state what students should know and be able to do. In addition to these standards that apply to all students, it is helpful to identify specific objectives for your English language learners. Incorporating goals, such as those listed here, will enable you to include ELLs in lessons and learning activities and ensure they are developing skills that will help them be successful.

- Students use verbal and nonverbal communication to express ideas, give and receive information, and participate in classroom activities.

- Students listen, imitate, question, and seek support and feedback from others as they learn to listen, speak, read, and write in English.

- Students practice their English language skills by using context to make meaning.

- Students learn to use English to follow oral and written directions, ask questions, participate in class discussions, and interact with others to accomplish classroom tasks.

- Students use English to gather information through listening, speaking, reading, and writing.

- Students use English to demonstrate knowledge orally and in writing and to respond to the learning of others.

- Students use learning strategies and skills across the language domains to understand and apply English skills to academic subject matter.

- Students observe, model, experiment with, and seek feedback about how to speak and behave in the classroom setting.

Q & A: Instructional Goals

The following Q & A addresses a few of the most frequently asked questions regarding instructional goals for ELLs.

What are the instructional goals for English language learners in math?

- ✪ Develop academic language skills in this content area.
- ✪ Develop an understanding of math concepts.
- ✪ Comprehend math vocabulary.
- ✪ Apply vocabulary and skills to solve problems.
- ✪ Organize their thinking about mathematics.
- ✪ Use the language of mathematics to communicate their learning orally and in writing.
- ✪ Analyze and evaluate the thinking and strategies of others.

How can I help my students meet math standards and instructional goals?

- ✪ Conduct a needs assessment at the beginning of the year or unit to determine students' familiarity with concepts.
- ✪ Post goals and objectives on the board to help ELLs keep track of and monitor their progress.
- ✪ Use advance organizers (pg. 38) to inform students of learning goals.
- ✪ Read through goals together as a class and have students restate the goals in their own words.

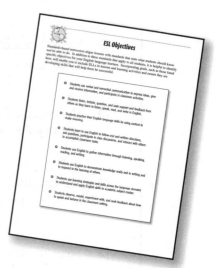

- ✪ Meet with students individually to help them develop learning goals.
- ✪ Have ELLs work with native English speakers to personalize goals.
- ✪ Determine the language skills that students will need for each lesson prior to teaching the lesson.
- ✪ Incorporate ESL objectives (pg. 11) into math lessons.
- ✪ Include how students will use math vocabulary as part of language goals.
- ✪ Offer study guides as appropriate so students can match their studies to stated goals and objectives.
- ✪ Differentiate instruction. Provide appropriate activities for each child to learn based on his or her educational background.

Q & A: Instructional Goals *(cont.)*

Which teaching strategies can I use to meet specific learning goals?

Learning Goal	Strategy
Develop academic language skills	Graphic Organizers (pg. 44) Sentence Frames (pg. 57) Small Groups (pg. 58)
Develop understanding of math concepts	Advance Organizers (pg. 38) Brainstorming (pg. 41) Mnemonic Strategies (pg. 50) Models (pg. 51) Peer Tutoring (pg. 54) Think-Pair-Share (pg. 60) Visual Aids (pg. 61) Whole-Group Response (pg. 62)
Comprehend math vocabulary	Advance Organizers (pg. 38) Graphic Organizers (pg. 44) Interactive Activities (pp. 45–46) Think-Alouds (pg. 59) Visual Aids (pg. 61)
Apply vocabulary and skills to solve problems	Asking Questions (pp. 39–40) Brainstorming (pg. 41) Interactive Activities (pp. 45–46) Multisensory Activities (pg. 52) Peer Tutoring (pg. 54) Small Groups (pg. 58) Think-Pair-Share (pg. 60) Visual Aids (pg. 61)
Express learning orally and in writing	Marking Text (pp. 47–48) Math Journals (pg. 49) Numbered Heads (pg. 53) Sentence Frames (pg. 57) Small Groups (pg. 58) Whole-Group Response (pg. 62)
Analyze and evaluate the thinking and strategies of others	Case Studies (pp. 42–43) Numbered Heads (pg. 53) Peer Tutoring (pg. 54) Reciprocal Teaching (pp. 55–56)

The Four Language Domains

TESOL's (Teachers of English to Speakers of Other Languages) language proficiency standards are divided into four language domains: listening, speaking, reading, and writing. They are listed in the order in which students become proficient. Below each language domain are activities targeted to support language development.

Listening

- ✪ Have students listen to other students explain their thinking in math.
- ✪ Have students hear more than one voice in English to develop strong listening skills.
- ✪ Have students follow along with a print copy when problems are read aloud in class. Students can underline words or phrases they don't understand for clarification.
- ✪ If possible, make audio copies of word problems available for students to listen to as they follow along with the print copy.
- ✪ Help students distinguish the sounds and meanings between math words that sound similar (e.g., many, money; than, then).

Speaking

- ✪ Speak more slowly and pause often.
- ✪ Use repetition.
- ✪ Paraphrase, if necessary.
- ✪ Have students express their thinking one-on-one or in small groups rather than in front of the whole class.
- ✪ Ask volunteers to talk through a mental math process to practice speaking.
- ✪ Invite students to explain to the class the math concept they just learned.

Reading

- ✪ Ask students to read directions or problems aloud for the class. Pair up students, if necessary.
- ✪ Simplify word problems.
- ✪ Help students understand the language of print in math textbooks, including complex sentence structures.
- ✪ Provide opportunities for students to read math-related materials.

Writing

- ✪ Review with students how to write numbers clearly.
- ✪ Have students write as they explain or share their responses with the class (instead of the teacher writing as the student talks).
- ✪ Give students opportunities to write about math.
- ✪ Have students write descriptions using math vocabulary.
- ✪ Model how to write word problems and explanations for solutions.

English Language Learner Instruction
Covering the Bases of ELL Math Instruction

Background knowledge, comprehensible instruction, and active participation are the "bases," or main components, of effective ELL math instruction. Accomplishing all three results in a "home run" of understanding for your students. Incorporate the suggestions and examples on the following pages when planning lessons to address the three major components of ELL instruction, specifically as they apply to math class.

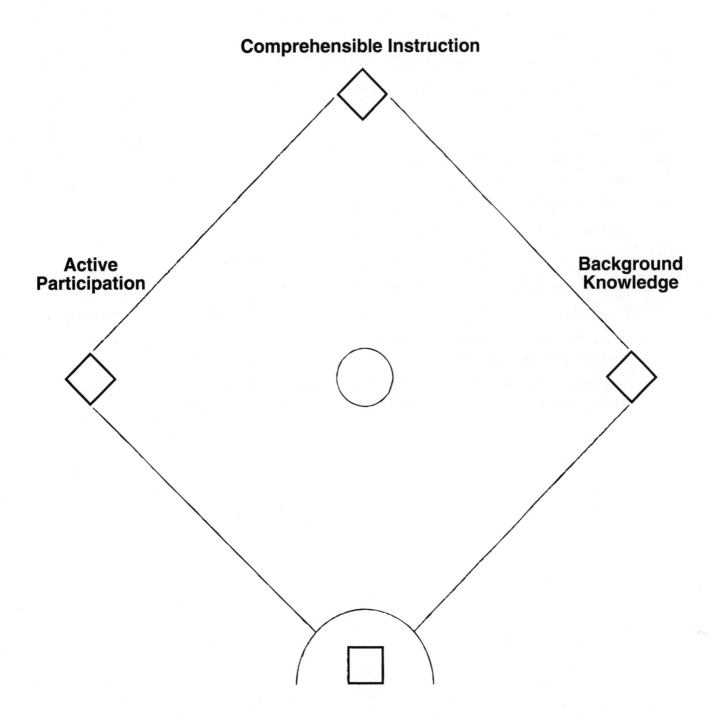

English Language Learner Instruction *(cont.)*
Covering the Bases of ELL Math Instruction *(cont.)*

Background Knowledge

What students already know about a topic affects how well they learn new concepts. Help ELLs access their background knowledge and make connections to relevant math topics by incorporating the following tips.

- ✪ Focus instruction with the purpose of building background knowledge.

- ✪ Connect instruction to what students already know and discuss how that knowledge applies to the topic at hand.

- ✪ Give students a strong conceptual understanding of the topic.

- ✪ Encourage students to use their background knowledge to help them understand new concepts.

- ✪ Draw on students' experiences during class discussions.

- ✪ Give students opportunities to use conversation, as well as reading, to build background knowledge.

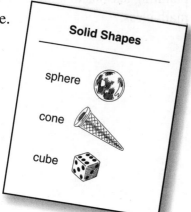

- ✪ Help students build background knowledge with sentence prompts, such as these:

  - ★ A time when I solved a math problem and felt good about my work was when . . .

  - ★ A time when someone helped me understand a math idea was when . . .

  - ★ A time when I helped someone else solve a math problem was when . . .

- ✪ Help students access the background knowledge they need to learn new concepts. For example:

  - ★ Students need to have a grasp of basic math facts (addition, subtraction, multiplication, division) to work with long division, fractions, percents, and decimals.

  - ★ Students need to understand sets and parts of a whole, data analysis, and how to represent and record sets of data in order to understand concepts of probability and ratio.

Comprehensible Instruction

Instruction is comprehensible to students when they understand most of what the teacher says. Incorporate background knowledge, present new information in context, and use visual aids to increase students' comprehension. Help students understand lesson content and activities by incorporating the following tips.

- Modify the curriculum as needed to ensure that ELLs grasp new concepts.

- Use language consistently.

- Simplify your explanations of new concepts before teaching new vocabulary.

- Include contextual clues, such as visual aids (pg. 61) and hands-on activities.

- Use graphic organizers (pg. 44) and study guides.

- Label pictures and diagrams.

- Help students make connections between English words and math symbols. Say each word while writing the corresponding numeral or symbol.

- Show students how to mark text (pp. 47–48) to help them understand new concepts.

- Adapt text.

- Allow students to use translation dictionaries.

- Allow for wait time, or time for students to think and respond to questions.

- Use preview and review activities.

- Give clear instructions. Write problem numbers and page numbers on the board in addition to giving the assignment orally.

- Allow students to clarify instructions in small groups (pg. 58), as applicable.

- Check for understanding with specific questions, such as these:

  ★ On which page can you find an example of how to do this problem?

  ★ What step do you need to do next?

  ★ Turn to a neighbor and explain to him or her what you just heard in class.

English Language Learner Instruction (cont.)
Covering the Bases of ELL Math Instruction (cont.)

Active Participation

Students develop English language skills when they talk. When teachers listen carefully to student responses, students learn that what they say is important. Meaningful interaction helps ELLs feel comfortable as they learn a new language and new content at the same time. Encourage student participation by incorporating the following tips.

- Increase teacher-student interaction.

- Use a conversational approach.

- Provide opportunities for verbal interaction in class.

- Ask questions and encourage students to ask questions.

- Encourage students to express their thoughts and opinions in English.

- Listen carefully to student responses and clarify, if necessary.

- Use math journals (pg. 49) to communicate with students.

- Provide ways for students to be actively involved in classroom activities (pp. 45–46).

- Involve students in lessons to help them remember content.

- Use an interactive whiteboard with pictures, diagrams, and text to involve students in lessons.

- Ask open-ended questions that do not have quick right or wrong answers to help students develop a process of thinking. For example:

  - How did you get your answer?

  - What else can you tell us about _____?

  - How is this question (problem) like the last question (problem)?

- Incorporate cooperative learning strategies.

- Allow students to work together to solve problems.

- Have students give and receive information and feedback as they work together to accomplish authentic tasks. For example:

  - Have students measure the temperature outside for a week and note the differences in the change of temperature.

  - Have students plan a garden on paper and draw a pattern of pavement stones for a walkway.

  - Have students graph school soccer-game scores to compare the overall season for two or three teams.

English Language Learner Instruction *(cont.)*
Recognizing Learning Styles

Students have many different learning styles, or ways in which they acquire information most effectively. Use the "Learning Styles Inventory" on pg. 20 to have students think about how they learn. Student answers can be used to guide lesson planning. Implement a variety of teaching methods, such as those suggested in the chart below, to expose students to many different learning and teaching styles. A diverse learning experience gives ELLs support while learning a new language. Have students work individually, with partners, in small groups, and as a class. Consider environmental factors, such as light, noise, distractions, and amount of workspace to meet student needs and learning preferences.

Teach to the Type

Visual	Auditory
Students learn and remember what they see. • Give students visual cues (pg. 61). • Use body language and facial expressions to communicate meaning. • Use charts, diagrams, graphics, pictures, video clips from the Internet, or DVDs. • Provide students with visual examples of concepts. • Use color to distinguish between different concepts in an explanation. • Encourage students to draw sketches to understand multi-step problems. • Use colored pencils, crayons, or pictures to show different parts of graphs.	**Students learn and remember what they hear.** • Allow students to say and hear problems aloud. • Have students talk with others to solve problems. • Communicate meaning with tone of voice and rate of speech. • Provide oral explanations. • Have students read textbook passages aloud. • Remove auditory distractions to help students focus. • Have students create their own acronyms and mnemonic devices (pg. 50) to remember steps in a process. • Have students talk out loud when solving math problems so they can hear their thinking processes. • Use songs to help students remember facts and concepts.
Kinesthetic / Tactile	**Sequential**
Students learn and remember through touching, feeling, and movement. • Use manipulative materials (pp. 32–33). • Incorporate movement to teach concepts. • Use gestures in class. • Have students draw cartoons to illustrate math concepts. • Act out the meanings of terms and concepts. • Have students physically move and arrange objects to demonstrate their understanding. • Have students create their own manipulatives to explore concepts.	**Students are organized. They plan their work and learn in logical steps.** • Have students work step-by-step. • Minimize distractions for these students. • Have students create diagrams of steps to solve problems and share with the class. • Have students make outlines to understand a problem or new concept. • Use puzzles to help students practice and understand concepts.
Global	
Students are spontaneous and easily bored. They see the big picture but may not understand how they arrive at answers. • Introduce lessons with information about how the concept relates to students' lives. • Allow students to see the whole concept, and then break it into parts. • Help students understand the connections within problems or how they arrived at their answers. • Encourage students to use drawings and different colors to understand the "big picture." Have students write their own word problems.	

English Language Learner Instruction (cont.)
Recognizing Learning Styles (cont.)
Learning Styles Inventory

Directions: Each statement below describes how someone learns. Add a "✔" next to the statements that are true for you. Your answers will help me plan lessons that will be easier for you to learn.

- ❑ I do well on assignments and tests when parts of them are read aloud.
- ❑ I can solve a math problem if I can observe how something works.
- ❑ I like to act out math problems.
- ❑ I understand a math problem better if I hear it read aloud.
- ❑ I like to discuss things in class with a small group.
- ❑ I remember what I see and read.
- ❑ Written instructions are easy for me to understand and remember.
- ❑ I can remember what teachers say if they use gestures or hand motions.
- ❑ It helps me if I can read a math problem aloud.
- ❑ I like to watch videos.
- ❑ Games help me remember new math concepts.
- ❑ It helps if I have something to look at when the teacher is talking.
- ❑ Oral instructions are easy for me to understand and remember.
- ❑ Graphic organizers (webs, Venn diagrams, etc.) help me organize my thoughts.
- ❑ It is easier to remember directions and other information if I copy it for myself.
- ❑ I like activities in which I can move things around.
- ❑ Drawing a picture helps me remember what I hear or read.
- ❑ A song or a chant helps me remember math facts or the steps in a math process.
- ❑ I like to read new information silently to myself.
- ❑ I like classroom activities in which we are involved.
- ❑ When we read together as a group, it helps me remember what we read.
- ❑ I like it when the math book has diagrams and drawings.
- ❑ When I learn something new in math, it helps me if I watch someone else work through the problem and then try it myself.
- ❑ I can understand a math problem better if we solve it together as a whole group.
- ❑ I can remember what I learn if I can make a model.

English Language Learner Instruction *(cont.)*
Engaging Students in Learning

Children learn more when they are actively engaged in their learning. Student engagement occurs at various levels: behavioral, emotional, and cognitive.

Behavioral

- ✪ Encourage students to put forth effort and participate in lessons.
- ✪ Model a willingness to accept not knowing the answer.
- ✪ Encourage students to plan and act for success in class.
- ✪ Consider the following: What can students do to help themselves focus?
  - ⋆ Experiment with different strategies to solve math problems.
  - ⋆ Work together in small groups and explain concepts to each other.

Emotional

- ✪ Help students feel comfortable with taking risks.
- ✪ Assure students that they might not find the correct solution at first, and that's okay.
- ✪ Give students confidence to try various strategies. This can be achieved by doing the following:
  - ⋆ Have them work with partners.
  - ⋆ Use peer tutoring (pg. 54).

Cognitive

- ✪ Provide opportunities for students to take ownership and invest in their own learning.
- ✪ Offer real-life math problems to generate student interest in finding solutions.
- ✪ Incorporate technology and multimedia into lessons (pg. 37).
- ✪ Provide online resources for students who need additional help.
- ✪ Consider the following: What helps students invest in their own learning?
  - ⋆ Offer a coaching environment in which the focus is on students and their abilities to discover and explore ideas.
  - ⋆ Model an interest in learning to motivate and engage students in the learning process.

Apply New Learning

- ✪ Have students check the teacher's work on examples.
- ✪ Provide opportunities for students to explore math applications in the world around them.
- ✪ Ask students to identify the implications their new math learning has for their everyday lives.

English Language Learner Instruction (cont.)
Establishing Cultural Connections

Math presents two challenges to ELL students: learning new math concepts and learning a new language. For this reason, it's important for teachers to acknowledge and accommodate English language learners' native languages and cultures.

Recognize native languages and support translation, as needed.

- ✪ Allow students to learn math concepts using their native languages and English.

- ✪ Use diagrams and other nonverbal representations to check students' understanding of math concepts and provide the new vocabulary needed for terms students already know and understand.

- ✪ Have students ask questions in their native languages. Translate as necessary to discuss in class, or have students discuss in small groups.

- ✪ Allow students to write in their native languages in their math journals (pg. 49). (They may have to translate for teachers to check their work.)

Acknowledge and incorporate students' cultures and backgrounds.

- ✪ Develop lessons and present topics that take into consideration students' cultural backgrounds. For example:

  - ★ Some countries teach the underlying reasons why a formula or procedure works, such as finding the area of figures or how to work with fractions.

- ✪ Encourage students to share how math concepts relate to their cultures. For example:

  - ★ Have students research and present information about mathematicians from their cultures, including the contributions these individuals made to mathematics. Consider one of the following mathematicians: José Ádem (Hispanic), Goerge Lusztig (Romanian), Luis Caffarelli (Argentinian), Henry Iwaniec (Polish), or Shiing-Shen Chern (Chinese).

  - ★ Conduct a class discussion in which students compare systems of measurement, problem-solving strategies, dates and calendars, or other differences they have experienced in math instruction.

- ✪ Encourage students to share things they do at home that relate to what they are learning in math. For example:

  - ★ changing the fractions in a recipe to double the amount or reduce it, converting a favorite family recipe from metric measurements to U.S. measurements (grams vs. pounds), reading a map, using money at a store, playing games (e.g., games of chance)

Cultural Differences

Different cultures use different sequences and approaches to teach math concepts. For example, students living in countries other than the United States learn different measurement units. When these students visit the U.S., they have to relearn measurement using English units.

In addition, many other cultures do not emphasize "showing your work," while some U.S. standardized tests require students to use words and pictures to describe how they arrived at their answers.

English Language Learner Instruction *(cont.)*
Skills for Math

Teach students the specific skills they need to complete activities and assignments. The skills provided on pp. 23–31 will help students in their understanding of math instruction.

Analyzing

Teach students this skill so they will examine problems more carefully. Breaking down multi-step problems into parts will help students understand how to solve problems.

Tips for Teaching the Skill

- ✪ Have students check to make sure they understand the words they are reading in directions or word problems.

- ✪ Teach students that to analyze a problem means to look at it carefully and understand what the problem is asking.

- ✪ Show students how to break problems into parts to determine the steps they will need to take to solve the problem.

- ✪ Make sure students recognize and understand the underlying structures of addition, subtraction, multiplication, and division (combining or increasing something, losing something, missing pieces, grouping, separating into groups, breaking apart) so that they can apply these operations in more complex math problems.

- ✪ Help students see that they need to organize their work and complete steps in the correct order in a multi-step problem.

- ✪ Help students recognize and eliminate extraneous information from word problems.

- ✪ Encourage students to analyze outcomes in probability tests so they can understand the results.

Sample Activity

Have students conduct a math investigation. They will analyze a situation to determine the information they need to know and the steps they will need to take to solve a problem. Consider sharing the following sample situation:

Twelve families want to establish a community garden. They have acquired a vacant lot that is 43´ x 121´.

Possible Questions:

1. How much fencing will they need to surround the lot?

2. How can they divide the lot so that each family will have a garden parcel?

3. What will be the size of each garden?

4. How can they separate each family's garden?

5. If Juan's family wants a fence around their garden, how much fence will they need?

6. If the boards are 6″ wide, how many boards will they need?

7. If the crossbeams are 8´ long, how many crossbeams will they need?

English Language Learner Instruction (cont.)
Skills for Math (cont.)

Clarifying

Teach students strategies to learn new vocabulary (pp. 63–65) to clarify meaning in math directions and problems. Encourage ELLs to stop and clarify when they read something they don't understand.

Tips for Teaching the Skill

- ✪ Encourage students to talk and write about math to clarify their ideas.
- ✪ Have students paraphrase, or restate, the problem in their own words.
- ✪ Encourage students to underline keywords and key phrases (pp. 47–48).
- ✪ Remind students to ask themselves what the problem is asking.
- ✪ Ask questions and have students ask questions to help them clarify their thinking.
- ✪ Give students feedback on their responses.
- ✪ Allow students to use their native languages to clarify concepts.
- ✪ Use graphic organizers (pg. 44) to clarify the meaning of a concept.
- ✪ Create a poster or other visual reminder to help students understand math concepts, directions, and problems. Consider highlighting the following tips on your poster:

> ✔ Re-read.
> ✔ Look for visual cues.
> ✔ Check the pronunciation and meaning of words you don't know.
> ✔ Read the context to understand what a math problem is asking.
> ✔ Clarify main ideas by highlighting keywords.

- ✪ Make sure students understand what to do during math activities.
- ✪ Help students clarify their understanding of the problem before they start to solve it. Have students use different colors to represent "what they know" and "what the problem is asking."
- ✪ Check in with individual English language learners after the lesson has been presented and have them repeat back the assignment or the process they will use to solve the math problem(s).

Sample Activity
Have students work with partners or in small groups to create concept maps to clarify their understanding of variables. Maps will vary but should be similar to the following:

Variables

We don't always know the number or amount of something.

Why do we use variables?

What is a variable?

A variable is a letter used to represent an unknown number or quantity.

Variables can help us solve problems.

English Language Learner Instruction *(cont.)*
Skills for Math *(cont.)*

Comparing and Contrasting

Teach students this skill so they can compare and contrast groups of numbers, equations, and geometric shapes. Have students use this skill to understand how math problems are similar or different.

Tips for Teaching the Skill

✪ Use compare and contrast diagrams to help students see the similarities and differences between sets of numbers or groups of information.

✪ Have students compare and contrast the steps in two processes (e.g., multiplying and dividing decimals) to deepen their understanding.

✪ Teach students to use compare and contrast to understand how and when to use equivalent numbers, such as fractions, decimals, and percentages.

✪ Have students practice their money computation skills by comparing and contrasting sales advertisements.

Sample Activities
Provide samples of different types and sizes of triangles for students to compare and contrast. Have students create charts explaining how the different triangles are similar and different.
Have students use Venn diagrams to compare and contrast types of numbers, such as decimals, fractions, and percentages.
Have students use a variety of standard (American customary system) and metric measurements to measure objects in the classroom (e.g., length of desks, weight of textbooks, temperature of classroom, amount of water to water a plant). Then have students work in small groups to compare and contrast the two systems of measurement. Consider asking the following questions: 1. Which system is easiest to use? Why? 2. Which measurement is more exact, and why do you think so?

Making Connections

Teach students that they are making connections when they use what they already know to understand new math concepts. Encourage them to look for ways in which they use math in their daily lives.

Tips for Teaching the Skill

- ✪ Help students make connections between concrete objects, pictures, diagrams, math symbols, and verbal expressions to make sense of math.

- ✪ Use manipulatives (pp. 32–33), such as buttons and beans, and drawings to help students understand concepts rather than just memorize steps in a process.

- ✪ Help students recognize connections between different topics in math to help them solve problems. For example, students use their knowledge of decimals to solve problems with money.

- ✪ Give students opportunities to explore problem solving and express their solutions in a variety of ways: graphic representations, with numbers and symbols, with physical objects (e.g., manipulatives), orally, and in writing.

- ✪ Remind students that they make connections when they use their math knowledge to represent real-world information (e.g., data from a survey).

Sample Activity
Incorporate math language when students participate in learning activities in other curriculum areas. Encourage students to use math as they complete projects. For example, as a social studies/math activity, have students compare and contrast the highest and lowest land elevations in your community or state. Students can construct graphs or write about how land elevations affect rainfall and other climate patterns, which in turn affects agriculture and other human endeavors.

English Language Learner Instruction (cont.)
Skills for Math (cont.)

Making Inferences

Teach students this skill so they can make accurate predictions, understand cause-and-effect relationships, and summarize information. Remind students that they make inferences when they use clues and what they already know about math processes to solve problems. Context clues such as explanations or details, along with students' background knowledge, can help students solve problems, make decisions, or answer questions.

Students make inferences in math when they do the following:

★ use their prior knowledge to understand what a problem is asking.

★ use the information given to figure out the next step of a problem.

★ complete steps of a process in the proper order.

★ sequence events to understand problems.

★ organize data for graphing.

Tips for Teaching the Skill

✪ Have students make predictions about what they think will happen when they manipulate objects.

✪ Help students use what they already know to make decisions about which strategies or math operations to use when solving problems.

✪ Demonstrate how to make predictions from data.

✪ Have students practice predicting the outcome of a series of events, such as a coin toss or the weather the next day.

✪ Have students predict the weight of objects (e.g., fruit, books, beans) and make weight comparisons.

Sample Activity

Have students collect data to create graphs. Provide step-by-step instructions for students to create their graphs. Model writing inference questions using an existing graph. The graph on pg. 28 can be used as a sample. Challenge students to write their own inference questions for partners to answer about their graphs.

English Language Learner Instruction (cont.)
Skills for Math (cont.)

Making Inferences (cont.)

Mr. Burke's fifth-grade class is doing a walk-a-thon to raise money for the school library. For 30 minutes, students will walk as many times around the school's track as they can. Students will ask friends and family members to pledge money based on how far they think they will walk or run. Look carefully at the graph to describe what happened when Caleb and Julian walked. Answer the questions below.

Caleb and Julian's Walk-a-Thon Results

Julian ———

Caleb ———

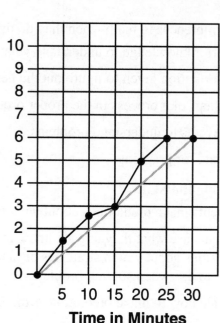

Number of Laps Around the Field

Time in Minutes

1. When is Caleb ahead? When is Julian ahead?

_____

2. When are they the farthest apart during the first 15 minutes?

_____

3. Describe Caleb's speed.

_____

4. Describe Julian's speed.

_____

5. At what point does Caleb catch up with Julian?

_____

Summarizing

Simply put, a summary briefly restates main points. Teach students that they are summarizing when they review, compile, or outline information. Highlight numbers, keywords and key phrases, or other significant details to demonstrate for students how summarizing can help them understand what a problem is asking.

Tips for Teaching the Skill

✪ Model and review how to summarize math content.

✪ Have students summarize lesson content with partners before working on problems.

✪ Give students opportunities to practice restating problems using their own words and pictures to demonstrate their understanding of what the problems are asking.

✪ Ask students to summarize the math lesson content—either what they heard presented or what they read in the textbook.

✪ Help students make the connection between taking notes and summarizing key concepts.

✪ Help students understand which information to keep and which details to leave out when they summarize.

✪ Tell students that they can learn to summarize by looking for patterns and synthesizing information.

✪ Help students practice analyzing content to summarize a math problem.

Sample Activity

Have students solve a problem or complete a math investigation. Have students share their solution strategies with partners. Students should then summarize how their partners arrived at their solutions. This will give them practice in restating the main points of solutions belonging to others. If desired, have students document the summary feedback from their partners.

English Language Learner Instruction (cont.)
Skills for Math (cont.)

Taking Notes

Teach students this skill so they can learn to summarize main ideas about math concepts. Notes can help students recall steps in a problem-solving process and other important information they will use to practice math skills.

Tips for Teaching the Skill

- ✪ Encourage students to take notes and add to their notes.

- ✪ Give students opportunities to review and revise their notes, perhaps as they discuss their learning with partners.

- ✪ Provide a cloze activity using a printed copy of teacher notes in which students can fill in keywords.

- ✪ As students take notes, have them draw pictures or other graphic representations to accompany keywords or concepts in their notes.

- ✪ Have students outline a section of text.

- ✪ Have students use graphic organizers to take notes.

- ✪ Use interactive whiteboard software, if available, to have students collaborate on taking notes and reviewing in class.

- ✪ Teach students various ways of taking notes, such as the following:

  - ★ Cornell notes (pp. 100–101)
  - ★ Outlines
  - ★ Graphic organizers (pg. 44)
  - ★ Notecards
  - ★ Marking text (pp. 47–48)

Sample Activity
Model how to take notes using one or more note-taking methods. Have students practice taking notes during math class. State which method students should use to take notes and have them use a different method on another day, or have students choose the methods they use and compare their notes with partners. Conduct a class discussion about topics for which each note-taking method would be most effective.

English Language Learner Instruction (cont.)
Skills for Math (cont.)

Visualizing

Teach students how to visualize so they can create math pictures in their minds. Students use their prior knowledge, known vocabulary, and understanding of math concepts to form mental images for problem solving and other math processes.

Tips for Teaching the Skill

- ✪ Use different kinds of pictures or graphics to help students understand math concepts, such as symmetry and the characteristics of geometric shapes.

- ✪ Use color to help students visualize numerators and denominators of fractions or place value of decimals (hundreds vs. hundredths).

- ✪ Model how to draw pictures and diagrams that show the relationship between parts of a problem.

- ✪ Translate problems into students' native languages, if possible, to help them draw graphic representations of the problem.

- ✪ Have students use manipulatives (pp. 32–33) as necessary to help them draw pictures or diagrams to represent the information in the problem.

- ✪ Use fraction bars to help students visualize problems working with fractions.

- ✪ Use photographs of objects of different sizes to teach ratio or have students create drawings to scale.

Sample Activity
Ask students to visualize a room in their homes. Have them draw diagrams of the rooms. Explain that even though they have drawings, students cannot actually measure their rooms during class. Instead, have students work together as a class to measure the length and width of the classroom. Ask students to visualize how the rooms represented in their diagrams compare to the classroom—is it smaller or larger? Based on the actual measurements of the classroom, have students estimate the length and width of the rooms in their drawings. If desired, have students check their estimates as homework.

Manipulatives, real-world math examples (discrete mathematics, mathematization), and technology are three instructional tools that can increase student comprehension of math concepts. These tools are especially effective with global, kinesthetic, tactile, and visual learners—learners who often need to see, touch, and connect with objects in order to understand them.

Students can use manipulatives to express math ideas and deepen their understanding of math concepts. Manipulatives give students confidence in their math investigations.

Tips for Incorporating Manipulatives Into Math Curriculum

- ✪ Make sure students understand the connection between the manipulatives and the math concepts presented in the textbook.

- ✪ Have students create manipulatives related to their interests, such as beads, sports cards, or bracelets.

- ✪ Use manipulatives to help students fully understand fractions and decimals before they practice computation problems.

- ✪ Use manipulatives to help students make the transition from concrete objects to visual representations (drawings or sketches) to using numbers and symbols.

- ✪ Use fraction bars (which are easier to visualize than fraction circles) to help students make the transition from visual aids to symbolic and numerical representations.

- ✪ Maintain a balance between using manipulatives and having students express math ideas on paper.

- ✪ Incorporate students' experiences with manipulatives into math writing assignments.

- ✪ Consider which manipulatives are most appropriate for each math concept. Use the following chart as a guide:

Manipulative	Use to Teach
geoboards	polygons, angles, area, perimeter, symmetry, congruency
tangrams	motion geometry, patterns
dice, spinners, playing cards	probability
play money	decimals
protractors	angles
base-10 blocks	fractions, decimals, place value
fraction bars or fraction pieces	fractions
pattern blocks	symmetry, angles, motion geometry, tessellations
boxes, books, or other objects and containers	perimeter, area, volume, geometric solids
interactive manipulatives or interactive whiteboards	shapes and lines (using a word processor or paint program), math concepts (using Internet websites with activities or manipulatives)

English Language Learner Instruction (cont.)
Instructional Tools: Manipulatives (cont.)

Sample Activities

- ✪ Place a variety of problems with manipulatives around the room in random order. Have students work individually or with partners to move around the room and solve each problem before moving on to the next problem.

- ✪ Set up an obstacle course. Students will complete various math tasks as they navigate the course. For example:

  - ⋆ Place a box as part of the course and have students measure and find the area of the box.

  - ⋆ Set up two or more containers, each labeled with a number. Provide several math problems on small slips of paper. Each problem should have one of the numbers as the answer. Have each student solve one math problem, crumple up his or her work paper, and toss it into the correct container.

  - ⋆ Have students complete small tasks that might take more than one minute but less than three minutes, such as sharpening pencils, distributing papers, and collecting library books. A partner or volunteer will time students with a stopwatch. Students should complete the task more than once and compute the difference between the two times.

  - ⋆ Have students solve relevant real-life money problems, such as how much money they would need to purchase various treats at the school bake sale or the most efficient way to buy school supplies given various packaging options (e.g., bulk, online) with different prices.

- ✪ Have students use manipulative materials to demonstrate and learn properties of equality.

- ✪ Find several diagrams related to a concept students need to learn or review. Assign each student a different diagram at random. Have students trace their diagrams on tissue paper from a printed copy or textbook. Encourage students to add color to their diagrams and explain them to partners.

- ✪ Have students use playdough (See below for recipe.) to make geometric solids, such as spheres, cubes, pyramids, and cylinders.

Playdough Recipe

- 1 cup flour
- 1 cup hot water
- 2 T cream of tartar
- $\frac{1}{2}$ cup salt
- 1 T oil
- food coloring (optional)

Stir together all the ingredients. Be careful! The dough is hot at first.

English Language Learner Instruction *(cont.)*
Instructional Tools: Discrete Mathematics

Discrete mathematics uses real-world examples to connect math concepts to everyday life. It helps students apply math and make it relevant to real life. These types of math lessons include concrete, visual, and hands-on strategies, which provide additional support for English language learners.

Students at all grade levels use discrete mathematics principles and applications, such as systematic listing and counting, vertex-edge graphs, and iteration (repeating patterns or steps in a process) as they learn and practice math. Use the principles of discrete mathematics to encourage students to find solutions to real-life problems.

Systematic Listing and Counting

Students practice this skill when they sort and classify information or objects. Creating an organized list can help students categorize information or determine how many combinations of different objects or numbers can be formed.

Sample Activity

Have students assist you with planning groups for small-group discussions during the school day. Give the problem a context by discussing with students how many students will be in a group, how many different times you wish to change groups, etc. Have students determine the number of different student groupings that could be formed. Add an extra challenge by specifying that students may or may not include friends in the possible grouping arrangements.

Vertex-Edge Graphs

Students use the concept of a vertex-edge graph when they color a map of the United States with four colors so that the same two colors do not touch each other. This is called four-color map theory. Students develop graphing skills when they find the best way to get from point A to point B or the closest location to a given point.

Sample Activities

- ✪ Relate vertex-edge graphing to a study of explorers. Propose that the explorers want to survey an area to create a new map but they do not want to go down the same path or by the river too many times. Have students create sample maps using principles of vertex-edge graphing and what they have learned about explorers' journeys and discoveries.

- ✪ Have students use four-color map theory to create a schedule for classroom jobs or computer time. Provide or have students create a table similar to the one shown on the next page. One chart represents a quarter of the school year. Each student group has a color. Challenge students to determine how the graph would change if there were five or six groups in the class or five days of computer time per week.

English Language Learner Instruction (cont.)
Instructional Tools: Discrete Mathematics (cont.)

Vertex-Edge Graphs (cont.)
Sample Activities (cont.)

Computer Time Schedule

	Day 1	Day 2	Day 3	Day 4
Week 1	(red)	(yellow)	(blue)	(green)
Week 2	(green)	(red)	(yellow)	(blue)
Week 3	(blue)	(green)	(red)	(yellow)
Week 4	(yellow)	(blue)	(green)	(red)
Week 5				
Week 6				
Week 7				
Week 8				
Week 9				

As a class, discuss ways in which students see these principles at work in real life:

- scheduling meetings for school clubs
- travel routes to get to a specific destination
- airline flying routes
- cell phone coverage with different towers and frequencies

Iteration

This area of discrete mathematics refers to the repetition of patterns or actions in a process. Students practice this skill not only when they work with patterns but also when they repeat actions in a process to reach a goal. Provide opportunities for students to use patterns to solve problems.

Sample Activities

- ✪ Have volunteers share when they did an action over and over again to complete a task (e.g., playing a sport or computer game or completing chores). Ask questions about the experience to investigate and extend the pattern. Translate the questions and answers into math symbols and number sentences. Have students make sketches to describe the pattern as needed.

- ✪ Have students brainstorm different ways in which they use patterns to solve problems. For example, who plays on which soccer team at recess or how to plan time for homework, chores, and fun.

English Language Learner Instruction (cont.)
Instructional Tools: Mathematization

Introduce students to the concept of "mathematization," or finding math in everyday experiences and expressing it in math terms. Relate math to other topics of study, such as quilt or wallpaper designs (geometric shapes), maps and travel (measurement), sports (statistics, time), game shows (probability), architecture (angles, measurement), sales advertisements (money), and bus schedules (time).

The following sample activities, which are organized by category, will help your students make connections between math and the real world.

Operations	Have students double (or triple) the number of ingredients needed to prepare a recipe.
Geometry	Have students analyze an animated film using the following questions: • How do artists incorporate geometric shapes into animated drawings? • What techniques help make two-dimensional objects look three-dimensional (e.g., characters, buildings)?
Measurement and Estimation	Suggest a situation to students in which a shelf will be placed on a wall of the classroom or a bookcase will be constructed. Have students measure, estimate, and calculate the materials needed, as well as find an appropriate place in the classroom to put the new shelf (shelves). Ask students which math skills they would use other than measuring (e.g., angles, geometric shapes). Have students discuss how time, speed, and distance are used in computer/video games. Then instruct students to design a game using measurement skills (e.g., include the distances in a treasure hunt, determine the water capacity in a water-sport game).
Money	Divide students into groups of three or four. Each group will act out a scene depicting how they use financial concepts in their lives (e.g., shopping at the store, earning money for doing chores, saving money, calculating sales tax). Have students figure out the different combinations of snack items, such as granola bars, apples, bottles of juice, etc., they can buy with a set amount of money.
Statistics for Fractions, Percentage, and Probability	Give students a sample weather forecast that indicates different chances of precipitation for the next few school days. Ask students to make a decision about which day they would rather have their class picnic, based on the weather report. Have students use the percentages given and explain their reasoning. Show students how to add their scores on various assignments and calculate an average to determine what grade they might receive in different scenarios. Have students work in groups to determine which movies had the highest and lowest percentages of ticket sales.

English Language Learner Instruction (cont.)
Instructional Tools: Technology

Use technology—such as software, demonstration videos, interactive sites, computer games, and Web 2.0—to help ELLs construct math knowledge. Because students are already familiar with these resources, the math concepts provided seem less foreign and more understandable.

Software

Go beyond software that offers basic math practice and incorporate simulation software that introduces students to math applications in real-world scenarios.

Sample Activity

Have students use Microsoft Excel or other graphing software to create graphs that depict the types of books, movies, or sports that students in the class enjoy.

Demonstration Videos

Use cameras and other audiovisual equipment to record videos that portray teachers and students completing math problems and engaging in other math-related activities.

Sample Activity

Use the record feature on an interactive whiteboard to document steps for a procedure, such as finding the area of a geometric shape or solving an equation with a variable.

Interactive Math Sites

These sites provide many resources for teachers, including games for practicing specific math skills, activities for interactive whiteboards, and math investigations. See "Websites for Educators" (pp. 107–108) for a list of recommended math sites.

Sample Activity

Use interactive math sites to post a problem of the day (or week) for the class, or have students experiment with patterns and tessellations.

Computer Games

Computer games can help students practice critical-thinking skills, increase their confidence and exposure to math concepts, and give students opportunities to use problem-solving skills. When computer games are one factor among many in a classroom that employs diverse teaching and learning strategies, some students may improve their scores on standardized testing.

Sample Activity

Use a puzzle generator to have students become familiar with math vocabulary as they complete word searches or crossword puzzles that incorporate new math words.

Web 2.0

Web 2.0 refers to that aspect of the Internet that focuses on content creation and user participation, rather than just surfing existing webpages. It includes applications such as podcasts, blogs, open-source programs, and wikis.

Sample Activity

Create a class blog on which students post their new math discoveries and how they are using math in their daily lives.

English Language Learner Instruction (cont.)
Teaching Strategies

Teachers use a variety of techniques, methods, and materials to help their ELLs meet learning goals and objectives. The strategies provided in this section may help students feel at ease in the classroom, participate in lessons, and learn new content at the same time they are learning a new language. Incorporate a variety of teaching strategies into lesson plans and classroom activities to address students' needs.

Advance Organizers

Use this strategy at the beginning of a unit to introduce key terminology and concepts. Preview questions and/or content to help students remember the lesson later.

Advance organizers help students do the following:

✪ understand how to think about the lesson content.

✪ think about what they will learn (new knowledge).

✪ compare what they already know with what they will learn.

✪ recognize patterns and think about relationships between concepts.

Examples

anticipation guide—distribute preview sheets with true/false questions about the topic so students can think about their opinions and ideas

concept map—illustrate the relationships between different parts of the concept

narrative—preview lesson content with a personal story or anecdote

questions—pose questions for students to think about

skimming—have students skim material and become familiar with specific content

web—use a web to introduce keywords or key points in lesson content before teaching

Tip for Teaching the Strategy

Use terms and concepts students already know to link to the new content.

Sample Activity

Display labeled pictures of different types of lines: parallel, perpendicular, intersecting, angles, and line segments. Have students draw concept maps to show their understanding of the relationships between the diagrams. Encourage students to include real-life examples of each representation. Conduct a classroom discussion to activate students' background knowledge and clarify misconceptions of the topic. Consider displaying the following example:

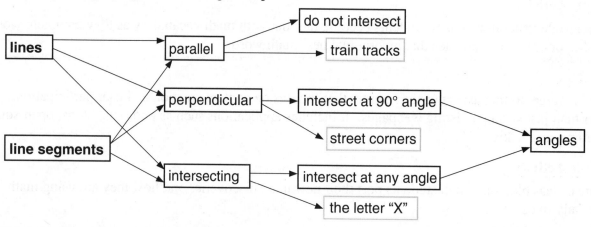

English Language Learner Instruction (cont.)
Teaching Strategies (cont.)

Asking Questions

Use this strategy to help students identify specific information. Asking questions, such as "why" or "how," helps students to develop their critical-thinking skills. Model how to ask questions so that students understand question structure and question-word meaning. Encourage students to ask questions when solving problems. Then relate those questions to the main math concept in the lesson.

Examples

gesture-eliciting questions—Make a triangle with an obtuse angle using your hands. What is it? *(scalene)*

yes/no questions—Are there any triangles that have two equal angles? *(isosceles)*

short-answer questions—Is a triangle with three equal angles an equilateral triangle or an isosceles triangle? *(equilateral)*

sentence frames—A scalene triangle has no _____. *(equal sides or equal angles)*

Tips for Teaching the Strategy

* ★ Ask questions that require students to explain their thinking.

* ★ Offer questions at various proficiency levels for English language learners.

* ★ Use different types of questions to differentiate and allow students to think and respond at their own levels (e.g., gestures, yes/no, short answer).

* ★ Practice wait time for student responses when asking questions in class.

* ★ Begin with foundation questions and then move on to building questions. Foundation questions give hints to help students clarify their thinking and determine which strategy to use. Building questions help students understand how problems get solved and give students insight into their thinking processes.

Foundation Questions	Building Questions
What do you know from reading the problem?	Why did you decide to use (addition, subtraction, multiplication, division)?
What is the problem asking?	
What other problems have you solved that were like this problem? What did you do to solve those problems?	What do you need to do next?
	What does this part mean?
What is another way to think about this problem?	Why did you . . . ?
What kind of picture or diagram would help you think about this problem?	How do you know your answer is correct?
	How do you know you have done everything the problem is asking?
What kind of answer would make sense for this problem?	What would happen if you changed part of the problem?

English Language Learner Instruction (cont.)
Teaching Strategies (cont.)

Asking Questions (cont.)

Sample Activity

Have students discuss the process to solve a math question, such as the following:

Sample Problem #1

Dakota walks her neighbor's dog each day. She walks around all 14 blocks in the neighborhood. She must walk the dog for at least 20 minutes. It takes Dakota 5 minutes to walk 6 blocks. How many times does Dakota need to walk the entire route to make sure the dog walks for at least 20 minutes? *(Dakota needs to walk around the entire route two times to walk at least 20 minutes.)*

---

5 blocks

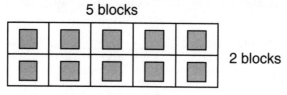

2 blocks

Route to Walk the Dog

1. Give students the information from problem #1 (above), but not the main problem question.

2. Model asking different levels of questions.

3. Have students volunteer the questions they would ask as they think about how to solve problem #1. Students are not yet solving the problem, just thinking about what it is asking and answering questions about the problem situation. Students could ask the following questions:

   - How far does Dakota walk if she walks the entire route one time?
   - How far does Dakota walk if she walks the entire route two times?
   - How many blocks will Dakota walk in 10 minutes? In 20 minutes?
   - What strategies can I use to figure out how to solve this problem?

4. Have students ask and write their own questions about problem #2 (below). Have them share their questions with partners and work together to answer both sets of questions about the problem. Students could ask the following questions:

   - What do I already know from reading the problem?
   - What do I still need to find out?
   - What does "149 fewer people" mean?
   - How can I check my answer?

Sample Problem #2

A well-known band from a major city put on three performances in your community. On the first night, 1,473 people attended. On the second night, 1,735 people attended. On the third night, 149 fewer people attended than on the second night. All together, how many people attended the performances? *(1,586 people attended the third night; 4,794 people attended the performances in all)*

English Language Learner Instruction *(cont.)*
Teaching Strategies *(cont.)*

Brainstorming

Use this strategy to activate students' prior knowledge or help them think about how to solve math problems. Have students think of as many answers to a question or ways to approach a math problem as possible, and then write down everyone's ideas.

Examples: webs, lists (e.g., ways to use math tools), clustering (about a concept), diagrams, word associations, categorizing information (i.e., grouping related ideas), asking questions (pp. 39–40), discussing strategies with classmates, drawing pictures to understand concepts

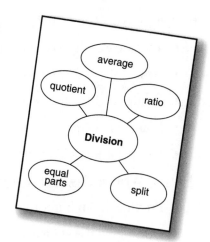

Tips for Teaching the Strategy

★ When compiling students' input, make sure everyone can see the diagram.

★ Encourage all students to participate. Model respect for all contributors.

★ Consider a small motivational incentive to encourage ELLs to participate in sharing their ideas aloud.

Sample Activity

Provide students with copies of a map of your state with a common scale, such as 1 inch = 10 miles. Have groups of students brainstorm strategies to use to find the total area in the state in square miles.

English Language Learner Instruction *(cont.)*
Teaching Strategies *(cont.)*

Case Studies

A case study is an in-depth investigation of a single group or event. Case studies are used to illustrate math principles or concepts. These problem-solving stories place math concepts into real-life contexts and help students make connections between concepts and problem-solving strategies.

How to Solve a Case Study (for students)

- Think carefully about the problem situation.

- Assess the information and determine what is known and which information is most important.

- While reading, ask questions that will help you think about the problem's solution.

- Make charts, graphs, or models to analyze the information.

- Use prior knowledge and experience, along with the information given, to solve the problem.

How to Write a Case Study (for teachers)

- Provide enough information for students to understand what the problem is.

- Don't give the students all the answers.

- Start by posing a question.

- Present some information in graphic form, such as graphs, tables, or charts.

- Pose ending questions and leave the conclusion for the students to decide.

Tips for Teaching the Strategy

★ Model how to ask questions that begin with "how" or "why" when students create their own sample problems.

★ Have students think of a problem in the school or community. What questions might they ask to solve the problem?

★ Remind students to think about the information they already know about the problem situation.

Sample Activities

Have students create their own story problems that include the concepts of division with a remainder. Consider sharing the following example:

> Derek and his family are moving to another house. Derek is packing books from his room into boxes. He has 39 books. Nine books will fit into each box. How many boxes does Derek need? *(He needs 5 boxes. All the books must go in a box; if he uses 4 boxes, 3 books will not fit.)*

Case Studies (cont.)

Sample Activities (cont.)

Provide students with a bar graph or chart and have them think of questions that the bar graph or chart would answer. Consider sharing the following example:

> Silver Mountain School was closed due to a storm. Now some of the students from Silver Mountain School attend Baker Creek School. There are more students now at Baker Creek School. The gym is used for lunch and PE classes. There are too many students now for all the grades to have lunch at the same time. The school needs a new plan to schedule how classes will share the gym. There needs to be one period after lunch with no PE classes so the lunch room can be cleaned.

PE / Lunch Schedule Before Storm

Class Period

	1st	2nd	3rd	4th	5th
9:40	PE				
10:20		PE			
10:40			PE		
11:20	L	L	L	L	L
11:40					
12:20				PE	
12:40					PE

Grade

PE / Lunch Schedule After Storm

Class Period

	1st	2nd	3rd	4th	5th
9:40	PE				
10:20		PE			
10:40			PE		
11:20	L	L			
11:40			L	L	L
12:40					
1:20				PE	
1:40					PE

Grade

Possible Questions:

- What are some of the changes in the PE and lunch schedule? *(4th and 5th grades have PE later; 3rd, 4th, and 5th grades have lunch later)*

- Why is there a class in the gym at 1:40? *(5th grade has PE)*

- In how many class periods was lunch served before the storm? *(one class period at 11:20)* After the storm? *(two class periods at 11:20 and 11:40)*

Graphic Organizers

Use this strategy to organize information, explain relationships between words, and help students see connections between ideas. Model for students how to use a graphic organizer so that they can connect new content to prior learning in meaningful ways.

Examples: word webs, semantic maps, compare and contrast diagrams (e.g., Venn diagrams), sequence charts, grids, organizational charts, T-charts, flow charts, concept maps, bar graphs, number lines, sketches

Tips for Teaching the Strategy

★ Adapt graphic organizers to match ELLs' levels of proficiency in English.

★ Use graphic organizers that show the relationships between words or concepts, such as factors and multiples.

★ Have students use webs to think about word definitions, ways they can apply a math concept to their lives, or how a particular concept connects to other math skills.

Sample Activities

Have students work with native English-speaking partners to create graphic organizers to show students in lower grades how to remember multiples and factor numbers. The practice will strengthen students' skills for additional work with fractions.

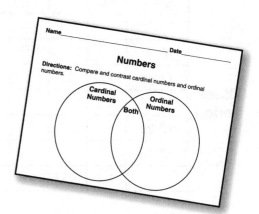

Invite students to create their own graphic organizers to depict their understanding of the relationship between math terms (e.g., sets of numbers—cardinal numbers, ordinal numbers, rational numbers, integers).

English Language Learner Instruction *(cont.)*
Teaching Strategies *(cont.)*

Interactive Activities

Students test their ideas and are exposed to different ways of thinking about math when they participate in activities with other people or a variety of materials. Introduce activities and integrate techniques that encourage interaction, such as incorporating math concepts into art projects, assigning quick-writes, or instructing students to survey classmates for data collection and graphing exercises.

Examples

Dialogue Journals

Have students exchange written expressions back and forth with partners, the teacher, or another adult aide or mentor. Assign various math topics for discussion.

Guided Lecture

1. Present the new information or math concept.

2. Have students take notes (pg. 30).

3. After students review their notes, have them share and discuss their notes in small groups (pg. 58) to check their understanding.

Interactive Lecture

Have students actively listen to the lesson. As they listen, they will do the following four things: (1) reflect, (2) stop, (3) write, and (4) give feedback to partners or to the teacher. Have students ask questions to clarify what they heard and help them develop their listening skills.

Interest Groups

Have all students work on mastering the same concept (e.g., practicing estimation) with different types of problems that are based on ability and interest levels (e.g., estimating time, distance, computations, money)

Pictorial Representations

Show students a graphic representation, such as a diagram or drawing, of a math concept. Do not include any words or explanations. Ask students to identify and explain the concept or problem-solving process represented. If desired, have students write about the concept using terms they have already learned.

Quick-Write

1. Pose a problem or a question.

2. Have students write quick answers.

3. Ask students to read their responses to the class.

Shared Input

Talk for 5 minutes, do a think-pair-share activity (pg. 60) for 2 minutes, then have students share as a class for 2 minutes.

Interactive Activities *(cont.)*

Examples *(cont.)*

Sketch to Solve

Teach students a series of steps to solve problems.

1. Sketch a picture or diagram.

2. Select an operation (addition, subtraction, multiplication, division).

3. Set up an equation.

4. Solve the equation.

5. Check to see if the solution makes sense.

Triangle Groups

1. Divide students into groups of three.

2. Have the first student read a math problem.

3. The next student will circle important numbers and underline the problem question.

4. Have the third student guide and lead a discussion among group members about how to solve the problem.

Tips for Teaching the Strategy

★ Have students demonstrate and describe their actions orally instead of, or in addition to, writing about their processes.

★ Have students use real-life materials.

Sample Activities

Set up a large representation of a number line. Have students walk along the number line to demonstrate various math concepts, such as the following:

- the commutative property of addition or multiplication.

- the identity element for addition or multiplication.

- the relationship between positive and negative numbers.

- how to perform arithmetic operations on positive and negative numbers.

Have students create math games for classmates to play. Games must have an obvious math connection related to one or more specific concepts learned in class.

Marking Text

Use this strategy to teach students how to mark text, or make notations, as they read. Marking text allows students to interact with what they read, increasing their comprehension. In a visual subject such as math, marking text helps students form mental pictures of what the problem is asking and develop appropriate strategies to find the solution. This strategy helps students do the following:

- ✪ comprehend what they read.
- ✪ notice patterns.
- ✪ identify what the problem is asking.
- ✪ identify relevant information needed to solve the problem.

Examples

underlining—emphasizing keywords, key phrases, or examples

highlighting—coloring specific vocabulary words and defining them in the margins

circling—emphasizing examples

margin notes—writing questions at the top of the page or margins to ask in class

sticky notes—tabbing pages, especially to mark equations or formulas often used

colors—using highlighters, crayons, or colored pencils to identify parts of a problem or different numerical operations within a problem

letters/symbols—coding parts of a word problem, including what the question is asking, relevant details or information, and irrelevant or unnecessary information

Tips for Teaching the Strategy

- ⋆ Give students a purpose for marking text.
- ⋆ Consider making photocopies of a text or math problem so students can mark freely.
- ⋆ Use clear plastic sheets over textbook pages or practice test booklets with washable markers.
- ⋆ Use scanners, document cameras, or interactive whiteboard technology to project copies of text.
- ⋆ Have all teachers use the same ways of marking text to provide consistency across grade levels or between leveled math classes.

English Language Learner Instruction (cont.)
Teaching Strategies (cont.)

Marking Text (cont.)

Sample Activities

Many students have difficulty extracting the correct data from story problems. Teach students how to identify the relevant information and differentiate it from the irrelevant. Use the following problem as an example. Have students mark the relevant text in one color and the irrelevant text in another color.

> Shawna is riding her bike at 6 mph. It is 12:45 p.m. She is 18 miles from home, and it is 70°F outside. What time will Shawna get home? *(18 miles ÷ 6 mph = 3 hours; 12:45 p.m. + 3 hours = 3:45 p.m.; Shawna will get home at 3:45 p.m.)*

Help students recognize that "and it is 70°F outside" is irrelevant information and should be marked a different color.

Provide copies of a math text passage. Have students read the passage silently and code it with symbols, such as the following:

✔ I already knew this.

* This is new to me.

? I have a question.

If desired, have students use different colors to represent the following questions:

- What do I know?
- What is the problem asking?
- Have I seen this type of problem before?

Have students share and discuss their remarks with partners or in small groups.

English Language Learner Instruction (cont.)
Teaching Strategies (cont.)

Math Journals

Use this strategy to help students make sense of new concepts and ideas in math. Students can use writing to think through the step-by-step process of solving particular math problems. Start by having students describe, in writing, how they solved a problem. Then progress to math-concept reflections, learning summaries, and free-writing prompts.

Ways to Use Math Journals

- Have students complete daily problems in their journals.

- Ask students to write daily journal entries, reflecting on the day's learning.

- Encourage students to ask questions they have.

- Have students complete specific assignments in their journals.

- Have students summarize a math concept in a journal entry.

- Have students use their journals for review.

Tips for Teaching the Strategy

- ★ Communicate your expectations for how students should write in their journals.

- ★ Model how to write a math journal entry.

- ★ Give students sentence stems to help them start writing about math.

- ★ Have students verbalize a sentence or two to a teacher, aide, or classmate, then write down what they just said. Continue this process to help students feel more comfortable with writing their thoughts.

- ★ Use prompts to guide students as they reflect on what they are thinking, feeling, and doing in math class.

- ★ Use a specific journal prompt to conduct a class discussion. Writing their responses before sharing in class will help ELLs clarify their thinking in English.

- ★ Refer to words posted on a word wall to use in free-writing prompts.

- ★ As time allows, give students written feedback on selected journal entries.

Sample Activities

Challenge students to create their own math puzzles and provide written instructions or descriptions for classmates.

Have students write on the same prompt and then share their journal entries with classmates for discussion or evaluation.

English Language Learner Instruction *(cont.)*
Teaching Strategies *(cont.)*

Mnemonic Strategies

Use this strategy to help students remember new information. Mnemonic strategies are most often auditory or verbal but may also be visual or kinesthetic. They may include keywords and/or illustrations to help students remember a series of words or facts. Here are the steps to implementing mnemonic strategies:

1. Provide students with the mnemonic device you want them to use.

2. Demonstrate and explain how to use the strategy to remember a particular fact or concept.

3. Practice with students to help them use the strategy correctly.

4. Give students opportunities to create their own mnemonic devices to help them remember math concepts with which they have difficulty.

> Remember that the numerator is above the denominator.
>
> **<u>N</u>ice <u>D</u>og!**

Examples: acronyms, acrostics, alliteration, names, models (diagrams), rhymes, poems, pictures, number chants or songs

Tip for Teaching the Strategy

Make sure students understand the basic concepts before teaching a mnemonic device.

Sample Activity

Have students create their own meaningful acrostics (oral or written) for the order of operations. Provide students with poster board or large pieces of paper so they can present their mnemonics to the class. If desired, have a contest for students to create the most memorable mnemonic.

Models

Use this strategy to help explain or describe math concepts to students. In math, models serve as examples of how things work in the real world; they help students understand the real-world application. Students can manipulate models to understand arithmetic operations, fractions, or geometric properties.

Examples: fraction pieces, base-10 blocks, pattern blocks, drawings, graphs

Tips for Teaching the Strategy

* ⋆ Keep models as interactive as possible.

* ⋆ Use manipulatives as models for objects (pp. 32–33). (e.g., Round counters can represent wheels in a problem about bicycles.)

* ⋆ Have students use blocks or other counters to model a series of equations when solving a problem.

* ⋆ Discuss students' observations of how the model works to illustrate the concept.

Sample Activity

Have students use base-10 blocks to guide them in making pictorial models to represent decimal numbers and place value. Allow time for students to practice using their models to solve simple problems with fractions, decimals, and percents. Have students keep their models for future reference.

English Language Learner Instruction (cont.)
Teaching Strategies (cont.)

Multisensory Activities

Use this strategy to engage students in nonverbal ways. Multisensory activities enable teachers to adapt lessons for different student learning styles.

Examples

Visual	Auditory
Have students create math problems from photographs. Use video clips to show the processes of solving long division problems using arithmetic algorithms. Use multimedia presentations to demonstrate concepts of data analysis. Introduce flowcharts to help students formulate a plan to solve multi-step word problems. Use color to help students organize their thinking.	Organize debates. Incorporate mnemonic strategies (pg. 50). Have students interview each other to explain how to solve an equation with a variable. Have students role-play how they would solve different types of problems. Use an interactive whiteboard to provide manipulative models for students to explore properties of geometric figures.
Kinesthetic	**Tactile**
Have students use number and letter tiles to create equations. Use manipulative objects to demonstrate math concepts (pp. 32–33). Have students use geoboards to explore geometric shapes and the effect of change on shapes. Have students play active review games.	Use magnets. Have students make three-dimensional math models (e.g., a folded paper cube following a pattern).

Tips for Teaching the Strategy

★ Try to involve more than one sense in a math lesson.

★ Present word problems using multisensory activities.

Sample Activity

1. Have students trace the outlines of their shoes or other common objects on graph paper. *(kinesthetic/tactile)*

2. Encourage students to identify basic shapes within the outline, such as squares, triangles, or trapezoids, and figure out the area of the shapes. *(visual)*

3. Have students add the individual areas together to estimate an approximate area of the entire figure. *(visual)*

4. Have students discuss with partners how they arrived at their final calculations and conduct a class discussion to determine the reasonableness of students' answers. *(The estimated area should be less than the area of a square or rectangle drawn around the outside of the shape.) (auditory)*

English Language Learner Instruction *(cont.)*
Teaching Strategies *(cont.)*

Numbered Heads

Use this strategy so students can work together in groups to discuss a new concept or solve a problem. Here are the steps to the numbered heads strategy:

1. Assign each student a number. Consider whether you want students to work individually for a set amount of time or go straight into groups.

2. Give groups a problem. Allow them time to discuss the problem and solution(s).

3. After students have worked together to ensure that everyone in the group understands, randomly call a specific number to indicate which student in each group should share with the whole class. (Decide prior to the activity whether or not you want the person who shares to have the option of receiving help from the group when sharing.)

4. If a problem has only one correct answer, have other teams in the class use a simple signal to indicate whether they agree or disagree with the given answer.

Ways to Use Numbered Heads: when teaching word problems or math relationships, discussing new math concepts, reviewing for a quiz or test

Tips for Teaching the Strategy

★ Have each group share one part of the answer for multi-step problems.

★ Select three volunteers to help you model for the class how to work together to make sure everyone in the group fully understands the problem or concept.

Sample Activity

Have students work together to solve a multi-step word problem. Assign one part of the problem to each member of the group. Encourage each member to identify the implied question—or information that needs to be determined—in his or her part of the problem. At the end of the activity, have groups share their thinking processes, or how they arrived at their solutions. Consider displaying the following example:

Student 1: Lily walks 250 feet per minute. Her bus stop is 5 minutes away from her house. *(How far is it from Lily's house to the bus stop?)* *(250 fpm x 5 minutes = 1,250 feet)*

Student 2: Lily's bus travels 2,000 feet per minute. It takes the bus 12 minutes to get from Lily's bus stop to school. *(How far is it from the bus stop to the school?)* *(2,000 fpm x 12 minutes = 24,000 feet)*

Student 3: Lily then walks for 2 minutes to get to her classroom. *(How far is it from the bus to her classroom?)* *(250 fpm x 2 minutes = 500 feet)*

Student 4: What do we need to do to find the answers to the final questions? *(combine answers from other members of the group)*

1. How many feet is it from Lily's home to her classroom? *(1,250 + 24,000 + 500 = 25,750 feet)*

2. How many minutes does it take for Lily to get to her classroom from her house? *(5 + 12 + 2 = 19 minutes)*

3. How many miles is it from Lily's house to school? *(5,280 feet in a mile; 25,750 ÷ 5,280 = 4.88 miles or about 5 miles)*

English Language Learner Instruction (cont.)
Teaching Strategies (cont.)

Peer Tutoring

Use this strategy to train students in instructional methods so they can help one another. Peer tutoring should be used with content that has already been taught in class. Have one partner "teach" the material and give feedback to the other. At a signal, partners switch roles.

Ways to Use Peer Tutoring

- Tell your students to be aware of when their partners start to have trouble.
- Have partners repeat back to check for understanding.
- Instruct students to explain how to find the answer.
- Advise students to ask their partners for help more than once (if needed).
- Encourage students to ask questions to clarify vocabulary.
- Remind students to not give the answers directly to their partners.
- Have students encourage their partners to explain their thinking and answers.
- Tell students to create an explanation of how to do the problem.
- Have students use drawings or manipulative objects (pp. 32–33).
- Make sure that each tutoring partnership is appropriate and beneficial. Use the table below as a guide.

Need	Tutor	Tutee
translate, learn new vocabulary, ask questions to give partners experience explaining answers	highly skilled	less skilled
translate, learn new vocabulary	ELL student—same proficiency level	ELL student—same proficiency level
assistance learning English	native English speaker	ELL student
learn new math skills, ask questions to give partner experience explaining answers	higher-grade-level student	lower-grade-level student
discuss new math concepts	random partner	random partner
practice with math skills	random partner	random partner

Tips for Teaching the Strategy

- ⋆ Identify one learning objective and review with the class to help students focus on the task at hand.
- ⋆ Establish signals that partners can use when one person needs help.
- ⋆ Give tutors prompts to use.

Sample Activity

Have students work as "experts" to help each other set up equations with variables. Give each pair of students two problems to set up. Have the first tutor help his or her partner set up the first sample problem. When students switch roles, the tutor will help his or her partner set up an equation for the second sample problem. Have students ask each other questions to clarify understanding, as needed. Encourage students to explain their thinking to their partners.

English Language Learner Instruction *(cont.)*
Teaching Strategies *(cont.)*

Reciprocal Teaching

Reciprocal teaching takes the form of a dialogue between students and teachers. Teachers and students take turns summarizing, generating questions, and clarifying. Once this strategy has been modeled, it can also be used in small groups with various students assuming the role of "group leader." Here are the steps to reciprocal teaching*:

1. Present an interactive lesson.

2. Introduce the text and have students participate in a discussion of the text.

3. Evaluate and monitor student responses for comprehension.

4. Restructure and reteach as necessary to correct student understanding and responses.

*Experiment with changing the order of the steps to fit different tasks in math class, such as reading text, solving word problems, or understanding new math concepts.

Examples

Summarizer	Questioner
identifies keywords or key phrases	asks questions to help classmates understand text
restates the most important points in his or her own words	asks teammates to verbalize questions they had as they listened to the lesson or text
includes keywords in summary	helps teammates think about the problem and what it is asking
asks teammates to summarize what they heard	
guides group reflection to make sure the problem was solved to answer the main question	

Clarifier	Predictor
makes sure teammates understand new vocabulary and concepts	sets a purpose for reading, using headings or subheadings and learning objectives
asks questions about unfamiliar words	asks teammates what they think they will learn next
points out parts of text where meaning may be unclear	discusses with teammates how understanding the current concept will help them understand the next part of the procedure or next lesson
identifies unfamiliar vocabulary	invites teammates to consider how this concept will help them in their lives
examines layout of text	helps teammates make a plan to solve the problem
highlights new concepts	

Reciprocal Teaching (cont.)

Tips for Teaching the Strategy

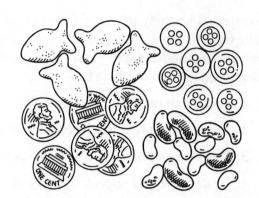

★ Model and help students learn how to generate questions that will help them in their learning.

★ Work with students to help them clarify ideas and new concepts, not just vocabulary.

★ Encourage the use of manipulatives (pp. 32–33), such as crackers and buttons, illustrate ideas, and increase student understanding.

Sample Activity

Have students work in collaborative groups to solve a sample problem. Consider reading the problem aloud or have one student in each group read the problem aloud. Assign student roles. Have students take notes throughout the activity on how they worked within the groups to fulfill their roles, as well as how their teammates helped them understand the problem and solution. Encourage groups to suggest tips for solving the problem, and then have them share their tips with the class.

Sentence Frames

Use this strategy to provide structure for students learning academic language. Sentence frames—also called sentence starters, sentence stems, or communication guides—have one or more keywords left blank in a sentence. Use sentence frames to do the following:

- ✪ help students learn new vocabulary in context.
- ✪ introduce complex math concepts.
- ✪ help students talk about math.
- ✪ help students understand word problems.

Tip for Teaching the Strategy

Create sentence frames based on real-world scenarios.

Sample Activity

Conduct a review activity at the end of a unit or specific topic of study. Arrange students in groups based on their understanding of recent concepts, with students who understand each concept grouped together. Have each group create sentence frames to help their classmates think through their understanding of the concept. If desired, provide a set of sample data to give students concrete examples as they create their sentence frames. Consider sharing the following sentence frames after students have reviewed *mean, median, mode,* and *range* (in groups, if desired):

- The mean is the _____ *(average)* of a set of numbers.

- I find the median by _____. *(listing all the numbers in order and looking for the middle number in the set)*

- The mode is the number that occurs _____ *(most often)* in a set of numbers.

- I had to find the mean once when _____.

- Use the _____ *(least)* number and the

  _____ *(greatest)* number to find the range.

- Find the range by _____ *(subtracting)* one number from another.

Small Groups

Use this strategy so students can ask questions and receive feedback and explanations in a supportive environment. When students work together in small groups, they can discuss different strategies to use when solving problems. The group works together to make and test a plan to solve the problem. This gives support to ELL students and enables students to experience and benefit from different ways of thinking about math.

Examples of Small Groups

blended—native English speakers and ELL students

bilingual—ELLs who can discuss concepts in their native languages as well as in English

fluency-based—more fluent students serve as assistants who communicate the lesson concepts (in English) to the small group and help guide the group discussion

skill-based—one or more students can share specific skills (e.g., vocabulary knowledge, background experiences) to help the group solve a problem

Tips for Teaching the Strategy

★ Give students specific guidelines to structure their work in small groups.

★ Prior to the small group activity, have a class discussion about group goals for learning.

★ Incorporate tasks and responsibilities for each group member.

★ Hold students accountable for their work both individually and as group members.

★ Have students rotate periodically from one group to another.

Sample Activity

Divide the class into groups of three to four students each. Give each group a different problem. Have students first work on their own to think about their problems. Have them write questions about the problems and what strategies they might use to solve the problems. Students will then work with their groups to solve the problems. Remind students to think about how they can explain their solutions. Have one student from each group form a new group in a jigsaw activity. Students will take turns explaining to their new groups how to solve their problems. Group members will take notes on the problem-solving processes and strategies used to solve the problems, as well as the solutions. If time permits, have students complete individual reflections on their learning in math journals.

Alternate Activity: Give each group a different task that contributes to solving a problem and have groups share their input with the class.

English Language Learner Instruction *(cont.)*
Teaching Strategies *(cont.)*

Think-Alouds

Use this strategy to show students how to think through the problem-solving process. In doing so, you model the steps needed to solve a problem. Encourage students to use think-alouds when reviewing concepts. Students can use what they know to help them reflect on how to solve new problems. Thinking aloud will help students remember the steps in a process and the order in which to do the steps.

Ways to Use Think-Alouds: when working with arithmetic algorithms; solving word problems, math investigations, and questions; figuring out possible solutions; modeling midcourse strategy changes

Tip for Teaching the Strategy

Record a think-aloud on an interactive whiteboard for students' future reference.

Sample Activity

Think aloud and talk through how to solve a sample problem, such as the following:

> Thirty people will attend the baseball awards dinner. They will be seated at square tables that seat one person on each side. The coach wants to arrange the tables with the sides touching to make one long table in the banquet room. What is the fewest number of tables he will need?

Possible thoughts: I want to see a picture so I can understand how this will work. I re-read the problem to see that the tables need to be arranged as one long table. Without a diagram, I don't have any guesses as to what the answer might be.

My plan is to draw a picture first. Then I'll either add or multiply—whichever seems easier based on my drawing—to arrive at a solution. This problem is similar to other word problems I have seen in which I would draw a picture to understand how to figure the least number of items needed in a given situation. I use the numbers (30 people total) and information in the problem to draw a picture. (Each table seats 1 person per side. The tables will be arranged as one long table.)

I number the people as I draw so I will know when I have enough tables. The problem states I need the least number of tables possible, so I place one person at each end of the long table. Then I count the number of squares (representing tables) in my diagram. I need 14 tables to seat 30 people in this arrangement of tables.

My solution makes sense because it is a picture of how the tables will be placed with numbers to represent the people. Drawing and counting is a slow way to solve this problem. I could have drawn just a couple of tables to see the pattern. Then I could write an equation to help me find the total number. There is a pattern that only two sides of each table (except the tables on each end) will have a seat. It works out to one less than half the total number. I could use the equation "one less than half the total" to solve a similar problem.

$(\frac{1}{2}$ of **x**$) - 1 = $ _____ tables needed

x = total number of people

$(\frac{1}{2}$ times 30$) - 1 = 14$

English Language Learner Instruction (cont.)
Teaching Strategies (cont.)

Think-Pair-Share

Use this strategy so ELLs can rehearse what they want to say, negotiate meaning with partners, and expand or correct their understanding. Here are the steps to think-pair-share:

1. Pose a question or problem for students to think about.

2. Give students a set amount of time to think (e.g., one or two minutes). If desired, display the question, problem, or diagram for student reference. Students may write their responses before they share with partners.

3. Pair up students to discuss and develop their ideas. You may wish to give students the option to discuss without finding the solution at this point. Encourage them to think about how they would solve the problem.

4. Call on a few students to share their responses with the class.

Ways to Use Think-Pair-Share: reviewing a new topic, brainstorming (pg. 41) how to solve a problem, summarizing what a word problem is asking

Tips for Teaching the Strategy

★ Assign partners at the beginning of the lesson.

★ Time students as they take turns sharing with partners.

★ Change partners for different lessons.

Sample Activity

Display a cube and a rectangular prism. Have students write words, use numbers and symbols, or draw pictures to think about how they would determine the volume, in cubic inches, for each shape. Have them discuss with partners which strategy is easiest for them to use and why. If time permits, provide one or two sample problems for students to solve using the strategy. Students may then share their answers with their partners.

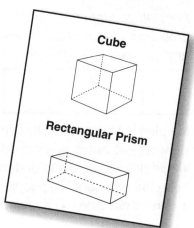

Cube

Rectangular Prism

English Language Learner Instruction *(cont.)*
Teaching Strategies *(cont.)*

Visual Aids

Use this strategy to help students solve problems while supporting students' language development. Use visual aids to help students clarify meaning and relate new vocabulary and concepts to graphic representations.

Examples: charts, diagrams, graphs, pictures, video clips, gestures, outlines, posters, flash cards, word lists, fraction bars

Tip for Teaching the Strategy

 ★ Have students create their own visual aids, such as fraction bars.

 ★ Use clip art or simple line drawings from the Internet to illustrate various math problems and concepts.

 ★ Use the capture feature of an interactive whiteboard to save diagrams developed in class as screenshots for future use.

Sample Activity

Assign a color to each operation, including exponents, multiplication, division, addition, and subtraction. Have students use color to create a visual aid showing the order of operations. The following is a sample key:

---

1. **Parenthetical** (operations within parentheses) = red

2. **Exponential** (raising to powers or finding square roots) = orange

3. **Multiplication and Division** (left to right) = yellow

4. **Addition and Subtraction** (left to right) = blue

English Language Learner Instruction (cont.)
Teaching Strategies (cont.)

Whole-Group Response

Use this strategy to emphasize particular points, review information, or elicit responses from students during lessons. Whole-group response also provides opportunities for informal assessment during class. Have students respond together as a group verbally, in writing, or with movement.

This strategy is also helpful for struggling ELLs who are less inclined to answer independently. In answering with their peers, ELLs feel less pressure and are more likely to participate.

Examples: choral response; response cards; individual whiteboards; interactive whiteboard personal response systems; gestures, such as thumbs up or thumbs down; physical movements, such as standing up or sitting down; chants

Tip for Teaching the Strategy

Have students echo back a word or phrase to learn new vocabulary and pronunciation of math terms.

Sample Activities

Use whole-group response with individual whiteboards, response cards, or an interactive whiteboard response system to review the temperatures for freezing, boiling, and normal body temperature using the Fahrenheit and Celsius scales. Pose problems that require students to use their knowledge of these temperature points, and then review the problems as a class.

To help students remember word meanings, have them act out or suggest movements for specific math terms, such as types of triangles, order of operations, or properties of addition and multiplication (commutative, associative, and distributive).

Math Language Connections
Vocabulary

Math introduces students to new vocabulary, terms, phrases, and sentence structures. Understanding these math language connections helps students think about math and comprehend new concepts.

Vocabulary instruction includes teaching students math-specific definitions of words, as well as how to use the new math vocabulary they are learning. Learning the language structures used in math will help students experience success in other academic areas as well.

Tips for Teaching Math Vocabulary

- ✪ Provide language acquisition support to help students learn new math terms.

- ✪ Use students' primary languages when possible to teach math terms and make connections to English.

- ✪ Teach students the language structures they need to learn math vocabulary. For example, provide sentence stems to place new words in a sentence or to use new vocabulary in context.

- ✪ Teach a concept prior to introducing students to the math language that supports the concept. For example, have students participate in an activity similar to "What's My Rule?" Using the whiteboard, place a card with two congruent shapes in one column and another card with incongruent shapes in a second column. Repeat with other congruent and incongruent items and see if students can determine your classification scheme. Then teach the related vocabulary.

- ✪ Help students understand the new ideas and concepts underlying the vocabulary words; they need to understand more than just the definitions.

- ✪ Give students opportunities to see and use the vocabulary in multiple contexts (e.g., by changing the wording slightly).

- ✪ Introduce vocabulary with descriptions and examples. Use the "Glossary: Math Terms" (pp. 66–72) and "Glossary: Math Verbs" (pp. 73–74) as guides.

- ✪ Teach math symbols along with accompanying vocabulary.

- ✪ Have students keep lists of new vocabulary words for their own reference when they work on math problems.

- ✪ Teach math-specific definitions for common multiple-meaning math terms (e.g., *root, face, mean, prime*).

- ✪ Inform students of math phrases that form a new concept by combining two or more words (e.g., *closed figure, decimal point*).

- ✪ Create word posters with cartoons, symbols, and/or mnemonics to help students learn and remember math vocabulary.

- ✪ Use a word wall as a springboard for discussions about new concepts.

- ✪ Use word association charts or diagrams to help students connect math terms and concepts.

- ✪ Use a modified T-chart to help students compare and contrast how words are used in math class and in everyday life (e.g., *point, product, sample*).

- ✪ Use academic journals to help students build meaning.

Actions to Improve Students' Vocabulary

The chart below includes actions that teachers and students can execute in order to improve students' vocabulary.

What Teachers Can Do	What Students Can Do
Use explicit instruction to teach new vocabulary each day. Include the following steps: • Say a word. • Write the word while reading it aloud again. • Have students repeat the word or phrase together. • Provide opportunities for students to use the new word or phrase again in a similar context. Give students structured opportunities to use new words in engaging and authentic contexts, such as conversations about specific topics of interest. Give students multiple exposures to content-area vocabulary before introducing new terminology. Identify when students already know the math concepts and just need the new vocabulary. Give students knowledge of root words and cognates.	Take a multi-step approach to learning vocabulary, which includes the following: • discussing what they read. • listening to words explained in context. • recognizing words as they're heard. Analyze new words using context clues. Develop study guides based on what they know about new terms and concepts, what they don't understand, and areas in which they need additional help. Talk with peers when they create study guides. Practice rephrasing definitions and explanations of vocabulary words. Practice writing sentences with symbols, numerals, and variables instead of words. Practice writing math expressions with words.

Math Vocabulary Activities

✪ Have students create definition cards with native language terms, English terms, definitions in their own words in either language, and math representations of the terms.

✪ Have students group words and explain how/why they grouped specific words together.

✪ Have students write down other words they know (not introduced during this lesson) and how they relate to the new word(s) they are learning.

✪ Have students keep files of note cards to explain math terms in their own words. Allow students to use their native languages on the cards.

✪ Create a template in Microsoft PowerPoint or another presentation program for students to use to express their understanding of vocabulary in creative (multimedia) ways.

✪ Help students build comprehension by exploring analogies in class. For example:

   ★ _____ *(cm)* is to *km* as *oz.* is to *ton.*

   ★ *Horizontal* is to *vertical* as _____ *(latitude)* is to *longitude.*

✪ Create a word map using the following format:

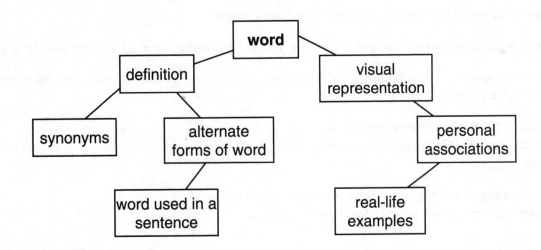

Math Language Connections (cont.)
Glossary: Math Terms

Math has its own jargon—a vocabulary that can be tricky for struggling ELLs who are still learning the fundamentals of English. ELLs may confuse the word meanings of multiple-meaning words (e.g., *mean*, *power*) or become frustrated when more than one math term is used in a sentence. (e.g., **Plot** the **ordered pairs** and **connect** the **points** in order.) To help them overcome these obstacles, copy the following glossary pages for each student in your class. Consider adding the "Glossary: Math Verbs" on pp. 73–74 for additional vocabulary help. Your students will feel more comfortable with this challenging subject if they have a math resource to consult.

absolute value: how far a number is from zero (Example: The number 5 is 5 away from zero, but the number -5 is also 5 away from zero; so the absolute value of 5 is 5 and the absolute value of -5 is also 5.)

acute angle: an angle that is less than 90 degrees

algorithm: a step-by-step solution to a problem

area: the amount of space inside the boundary of a flat (two-dimensional) shape, measured in square units

associative property: When adding or multiplying more than two numbers, it does not matter how you group the numbers. (Example: [3 + 4] + 5 = 3 + [4 + 5])

base (numeration): a number that is going to be raised to a power (Example: In 4^2, 4 is the base.)

capacity: the amount that something (e.g., a bucket, classroom) can hold

circumference: the distance around the edge of a circle

closed figure: a shape that begins and ends at the same point

coefficient: a number used to multiply a variable (Example: In 6x – 8 = 10, 6 is the coefficient.)

commutative property: When adding or multiplying, you can change the placement of the numbers and still get the same answer. (Example: 2 x 6 = 6 x 2)

compass (directions): an instrument that shows direction (north, south, east, west); its small, magnetic needle points north/south.

compass (drawing): an instrument with two arms, one with a sharp point and one with a pencil, that is used to draw circles

congruent: having the same shape and size

coordinate plane: the plane containing the x-axis and the y-axis

coordinates: a set of numbers used to show the position of a point on a plane

cube: a solid shape with six identical square faces

Math Language Connections *(cont.)*
Glossary: Math Terms *(cont.)*

cylinder: a solid shape with two identical flat, circular ends (bases) and one curved side

data: information or facts

decimal point: a dot used to separate a whole number and a fractional part of a whole number (Example: In 10.1, the dot separates the whole number 10 from the fractional number 1.)

degree (angles, °): a unit for measuring arcs and angles; a full rotation is equal to 360° (degrees). (Example: A right angle is equal to 90°.)

degree (temperature, °): a unit for measuring temperature

denominator: the bottom number in a fraction; it tells the total number of equal parts into which one whole is divided. (Example: In $\frac{3}{8}$, the denominator is 8. One whole is divided into 8 equal parts.)

distance: the amount of space between two places; the length of a line between two points

distributive property: Multiplying a sum by a number is the same as separately multiplying each addend by the number and then adding the products. (Example: 5 x (3 + 2) = 5 x 3 + 5 x 2)

dividend: in a division problem, the number that is divided (Example: In 12 ÷ 4 = 3, 12 is the dividend.)

divisor: in a division problem, the number that you divide by (Example: In 12 ÷ 4 = 3, 4 is the divisor.)

edge: the line where two plane surfaces meet

equation: a statement in which one set of numbers or values is equal to another set of numbers or values; an equation always has an equals (=) sign.

equilateral: having all equal sides

equivalent: equal in amount or value (Example: $\frac{1}{3}$ and $\frac{3}{9}$ are equivalent fractions.)

exponent (exponential): shows how many times the base number is to be multiplied by itself; it's written as a small number to the right and above the base number; it's also called "power." (Example: In 4^2, 2 is the exponent. $4^2 = 4 \times 4 = 16$)

expression: numbers and operators (such as + and x), and sometimes variables, that are grouped together to show the value of something

face: any of the individual surfaces of a solid object (Example: A cube has six faces.)

factor: a number that divides evenly into a given number (Example: The factors of 10 are 1, 2, 5, and 10, because each of these divides into 10 [10 ÷ 1 = 10, 10 ÷ 2 = 5, 10 ÷ 5 = 2, and so on].)

figure: a shape; a written number; an amount given in numbers

flip: a type of symmetry where one half is the mirror image of the other half; it's also called "reflection."

formula: a rule in math that is written with numbers and symbols (Example: The formula for finding the volume of a rectangular box is "V = W x D x H.")

fraction: a part of a whole number (Examples: $\frac{1}{2}, \frac{3}{4}, \frac{5}{8}$)

function: a way that two values relate to each other; every input value is paired with exactly one output value; it's written as "f(x)" where x is the value you give it.

graph: a diagram of values, usually shown as lines or bars

greatest common factor: the highest number that divides evenly into two or more numbers (Example: The greatest common factor of 18 and 30 is 6, because 1, 2, 3, and 6 are factors of both 18 and 30, and 6 is the greatest of those factors.)

grid: a pattern of horizontal and vertical lines spaced out evenly

horizontal: parallel to the ground; going side-to-side like the horizon ⟷

hundredth: one part of something that has been divided into 100 equal parts; it is written as $\frac{1}{100}$ or 0.01. (Example: One cent is a hundredth of $1.00.)

improper fraction: a fraction whose numerator (top number) is greater than or equal to its denominator (bottom number) (Examples: $\frac{8}{3}, \frac{7}{7}$)

inequality: a math sentence that says that two values are not equal; it is shown through the following symbols: ≠, <, >, ≤, and ≥.

integers: counting numbers (1, 2, 3), opposites of counting numbers (-1, -2, -3), and zero

inverse operations: arithmetic operations that undo each other (Example: Addition and subtraction are inverse operations.)

isosceles triangle: a triangle that has two equal sides and two equal angles

latitude: the position of a place north or south of the equator; it is measured in degrees.

least common multiple: the smallest number that is a multiple of two or more numbers (Example: The least common multiple of 5 and 6 is 30, because 30 is a multiple of 5 and a multiple of 6.)

line: a straight path that goes on forever in opposite directions ⟷

line graph: a graph that uses line segments to show how something changes in value (as time goes by or as something else happens)

line segment: a part of a line; it has two endpoints.

longitude: the position of a place east or west of the prime meridian; it is measured in degrees; lines of longitude are drawn from the North Pole to the South Pole.

mean: the average of a set of numbers; to find the mean, add all the numbers and then divide the sum by how many numbers there are. (Example: The mean of 2, 4, and 6 is 4, because 2 + 4 + 6 = 12 and 12 ÷ 3 = 4.)

median: the middle number in a set of numbers listed in order from least to greatest; to find the median, place your numbers in order from least to greatest and find the middle number; if there is no middle number, then average the two middle numbers. (Example: The median of 2, 5, 7, 4, and 6 is 5, because the middle number of 2, 4, 5, 6, and 7 is 5.)

mixed number: a number made up of a whole number and a fraction (Example: $2\frac{1}{4}$)

mode: the number that appears most often in a set of numbers (Example: The mode of 8, 8, 8, 2, 6, 2, 0, 7 , 7, 8 is 8, because 8 appears the most [four times].)

multiple: the product of a given number and a whole number (Example: 2 x 11 = 22; 22 is a multiple of 2 and a multiple of 11.)

negative number: a number less than zero

numerator: the top number in a fraction; it shows the number of parts from the whole (the denominator). (Example: In $\frac{3}{8}$, the numerator is 3. Three parts out of 8 are being considered.)

obtuse angle: an angle that is between 90 and 180 degrees

open figure: a shape that is not completely closed; it does not begin and end at the same point.

operation: a math process, such as addition, subtraction, multiplication, and division (+, –, x, and ÷)

order of operations: a set of rules that tells which operations should be done first; solve from left to right; use "PEMDAS" to remember the correct order: (1) **P**arentheses, (2) **E**xponents, (3) **M**ultiply and **D**ivide, (4) **A**dd and **S**ubtract.

ordered pair: a pair of numbers that shows the position of a point on a coordinate grid (Example: [3, 5])

origin: the starting point; on a number line, it is 0; on a two-dimensional graph, it is the point (0, 0) where the x-axis and the y-axis cross.

parallel: lines that stay the same distance from each other and never meet or cross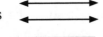

parallelogram: a shape that has four straight sides; its opposite sides are parallel and equal in length, and its opposite angles are equal.

percent (%): a part that is one one-hundredth

perimeter: the distance around a two-dimensional shape

perpendicular: a line that is at right angles to another line or surface

pi (π): the ratio of the circumference of a circle to its diameter; equal to 3.14159 . . .

plane figure/shape: a two-dimensional shape; it has width and length but no depth.

point: an exact location; it shows position but not size.

polygon: a plane shape (two-dimensional) with three or more straight sides (Examples: triangle, square, pentagon)

polyhedron: a solid shape with flat faces (Examples: pyramid, prism, cube)

positive number: a number greater than zero

power: shows how many times the base number is to be multiplied by itself; it's written as a small number to the right and above the base number; it's also called an "exponent." (Example: In 5^2, the power is 2. $5^2 = 5 \times 5 = 25$)

prime factorization: factoring a number into its prime factors only; it's also called "complete factorization." (Example: $18 = 2 \times 3 \times 3$)

2 x 3 x 3

prime number: can be divided evenly only by 1 or itself; it must be greater than 1. (Examples: 2, 5, 13, 19)

prism: a solid shape with two identical ends (bases) and all flat sides (faces); the shape of the ends gives the prism its name. (Example: A triangular prism has two triangular ends [bases] and three flat sides [faces].)

probability: the chance or likelihood that something will happen; it can be measured with a number or with words, such as *impossible*, *unlikely*, *likely*, and *certain*. (Examples: "There is a 60% chance of rain today," or "It is likely to rain today.")

product: the answer you get when you multiply two or more numbers

protractor: a semicircular instrument used for measuring and drawing angles; it measures degrees—from 0° to 180°.

pyramid: a solid shape with a polygon as a base and triangular sides (faces) that meet at a point on top

quadrant (circle): a quarter of a circle

quadrant (graph): any of the four equal areas made by dividing a plane by an x- and y-axis

quadrilateral: a plane (two-dimensional) shape with four straight sides and four angles (Examples: rectangle, rhombus, trapezoid)

quotient: the answer you get when you divide one number by another (Example: In $14 \div 7 = 2$, 2 is the quotient.)

range: the difference between the greatest and least values (Example: In 8, 9, 4, and 5, the least value is 4 and the greatest value is 9, so the range is 5.)

rate: the speed at which something moves, happens, or changes

ratio: a comparison of two amounts using division; shown with ":" to separate values, or as a fraction, decimal, or percentage (Examples: 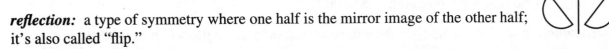 can be shown as 3:2 [for every three gray cubes there are two white cubes] or as $\frac{3}{5}$ of the cubes are gray, .60 of the cubes are gray, or 60% of the cubes are gray.)

rational number: any number that can be made by dividing one integer (counting numbers, opposites of counting numbers, and zero) by another

ray: a part of a line; it has a starting point but no ending point.

reflection: a type of symmetry where one half is the mirror image of the other half; it's also called "flip."

remainder: the amount left over when one number cannot be divided evenly by another number (Example: $17 \div 5 = 3 \text{ R } 2 = 3\frac{2}{5}$)

repeating decimal: a decimal number that has digits that repeat forever (Example: $\frac{1}{3} = 0.333 \ldots$ [the 3 repeats forever])

rhombus: a shape that has four straight sides of equal length; its opposite sides are parallel, and its opposite angles are equal.

right angle: an angle that is equal to 90 degrees

rotation: to move a figure around a given point; it's also called "turn."

rounding: reducing the amount of digits in a number while trying to keep its value similar; can round up or round down to the nearest ten, hundred, thousand, and so on

sample: a selection taken from a larger group; you examine it to learn something about the larger group.

scale: the relationship between distances on maps and actual distances; a machine used to weigh people or objects

scalene triangle: a triangle with no equal sides or equal angles

slide: to move a figure without flipping or turning it; the figure looks the same but is in a different place; it's also called "translation." (Example: You slide a checker on a checkerboard.)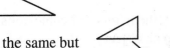

solid figure: a three-dimensional shape (Examples: sphere, cylinder, pyramid)

sphere: a solid round shape; every point on the surface of the shape is the same distance from the center.

statistics: the study of data, including how to collect, summarize, and present it

surface area: the total area of all the surfaces of a solid (Example: The surface area of a cube is $6e^2$.)

symmetry: a balanced arrangement of parts on either side of a line or around a central point

tenth: one part of something that has been divided into 10 equal parts; it is written as $\frac{1}{10}$ or 0.1. (Example: One dime is a tenth of $1.00.)

terminating decimal: a decimal number that has digits that do not go on forever (Examples: 0.75 [has two decimal digits] and 6.875 [has three decimal digits])

tessellation: a pattern made of identical shapes; the shapes must fit together (and not overlap) without any gaps.

thousandth: one part of something that has been divided into 1,000 equal parts; it is written as $\frac{1}{1000}$ or 0.001. (Example: One cent is a thousandth of $10.00.)

three-dimensional: a solid shape that has three dimensions, such as length, width, and height (Examples: sphere, cylinder, pyramid)

transformation: moving a shape so that it is in a different position but still has the same size, area, angles, and line lengths (Examples: turns, flips, and slides)

translation: to move a figure without flipping or turning it; the figure looks the same but is in a different place; it's also called "slide." (Example: You slide a checker on a checkerboard.)

trapezoid: a shape that has four straight sides; only one pair of opposite sides is parallel.

turn: to move a figure around a given point; it's also called "rotation."

two-dimensional: a flat shape that only has two dimensions, such as width and height; it has no depth. (Examples: circle, rectangle, triangle)

variable: a symbol used for an unknown number; it is usually a letter, such as "x" or "y." (Example: In the equation $4x + 5 = 21$, x is the variable.)

vertex: a point where two or more straight lines meet; it's also called a "corner."

vertical: upright, or straight up and down

volume: the number of cubic units (cubes) that it takes to fill up an object

x-axis: the line on a graph that runs horizontally (side-to-side) through zero

y-axis: the line on a graph that runs vertically (straight up and down) through zero

Math Language Connections (cont.)
Glossary: Math Verbs

In math, students are often asked to accomplish specific tasks. The verbs, or actions, used in directions may be unclear because the words are unknown or have multiple meanings. An understanding of what the directions ask will help students feel more comfortable with math in general. Consider photocopying these pages and attaching them to the "Glossary: Math Terms" on pp. 66–72 so that students have a complete glossary that they can reference.

calculate: to find something (e.g., number, answer) by using a math process (Example: Roberto calculated how long it would take him to wash the dishes.)

choose: to pick out something from a group (Example: You want to choose the correct answers when you take a test.)

combine: to put two or more things together (Example: For the equation $12 + 4x - 2x = 24$, you can combine like terms by subtracting 2x from 4x.)

compare: to show how two or more things are similar to or different from each other

compute: to find something (e.g., number, answer) by using a math process (Example: The baseball fan computed the player's batting average.)

connect: to join together two or more things

create: to make something

determine: to learn something by getting information

divide (÷): to split into equal parts or groups; it is "fair sharing." (Example: There are six tangerines, and two friends want to share them. How do they divide the fruit? Each friend gets three tangerines because $6 ÷ 2 = 3$.)

eliminate: to leave out or get rid of, as in to eliminate one possibility from among several

estimate: to make an informed guess about an amount, distance, or cost of something

evaluate: to look at something and think about its value

examine: to look at something carefully in order to learn more about it

explain: to make something clear so that it is easy for someone else to understand; to give a reason or answer for something

find: to discover, see, or get something

graph: to make a diagram of values, usually shown as lines or bars

identify: to correctly name something

intersect: to meet or cross something; intersecting lines meet or cross each other.

locate: to find

multiply (x): to add a number to itself a certain number of times (Example: Riley earns an allowance of $8.00 per week, which she saves. It's been three weeks. How much money has Riley saved? Riley has saved $24.00 because $8.00 x 3 = $24.00.)

Math Language Connections *(cont.)*
Glossary: Math Verbs *(cont.)*

organize: to put in order

plot: to draw on a map or graph

predict: to say that something will or might happen in the future

record: to write down information or facts

round: to increase or decrease a number to the nearest whole number, tenth, hundredth, etc. (Example: He rounded 3.7 up to 4 and 8.2 down to 8.)

select: to choose something from a group (Example: You want to select the correct answers when you take a test.)

show: to tell someone how to do something by explaining it in words, writing, or with actions

simplify: to rewrite a fraction or equation in a simpler form (Examples: $\frac{36}{48} = \frac{3}{4}$; $2 [x + 4] = 2x + 8$)

solve: to find the correct answer to a problem or question

Math Language Connections (cont.)
Confusing Language Patterns

One of the reasons ELLs struggle with math is that it contains confusing language patterns. Some of the most troublesome language patterns are listed below.

Language Pattern	Example	Remedy
Passive sentence structure	*What <u>is</u> the average number of buttons <u>worn</u> by each classmate?* *How many different ways can the ice-cream scoops <u>be stacked</u>?* *What <u>was</u> the total number of pie slices <u>eaten</u>?*	Rewrite as an equation by talking through the sentence phrase by phrase to help students match phrases to math symbols. *Each classmate wore _____ (average number) buttons.*
Misleading order (Students cannot always write the numbers and symbols in math problems in the order in which they are read.)	*Take 3 from 5.* *32 divided by 8 is _____ .*	Have students identify the math operation first and then structure an equation based on what they know about that operation. *Take/from = subtraction* *5 – 3 = 2*
Multiple-meaning words	*How many <u>faces</u> are on a cube?*	Reword the problem and discuss what it is asking. *How many surfaces does a cube have?*
The word "of" in fraction problems	*What percent <u>of</u> 180 is 54?*	Review how the word "of" relates to the concept of equal groups in multiplication. Then rewrite the question as an equation. *180 x _____ % = 54* Help students understand that they may have to rephrase the equation as a division problem to arrive at a solution.
Long or awkward phrases	*Find the sum of the length of all the sides of the figure.*	Break the problem into parts and then ask questions. 1) *Find the sum.* 2) Ask, "What do I need to find?" *the length* 3) Ask, "How many sides do I need to look at?" *all sides*

Math Language Connections *(cont.)*
Cracking the Code: Word Problems

When teaching word problems, it's important to start at the beginning. Students need to develop language skills and become familiar with this type of problem. Review common keywords with your students using pg. 78. Be aware of the main areas in which students have difficulty solving word problems. (See pg. 77.) Building a safe environment where students can take risks and try again will increase student confidence. The following tips will help make word problems comprehensible for your students.

Tips for Teaching Word Problems

✪ Relate sample problems to students' interests, prior knowledge, backgrounds, or current topics of study.

✪ Remind students to read a problem more than once.

✪ Read problems aloud and have students rephrase in their own words.

✪ Encourage students to take time to think about a problem.

✪ Clarify students' understanding of arithmetic operations, computations, and procedures.

✪ Help students think about the best plan or strategy for solving a word problem. After all, they may not see the answer immediately.

✪ Model and ask questions instead of telling students which steps they need to take.

✪ Ask questions, such as the following, that encourage students to think about the problem:

 ★ How could you try to solve this problem?

 ★ How can you break this problem down into smaller steps?

 ★ What are you thinking when you look at (these numbers/this problem)?

✪ Encourage students to notice the structure of the problem and compare it to similar problems they have solved in the past.

✪ Use a variety of ways to have students share verbally in class (turn and talk to partners, think-pair-share, small groups, whole class).

✪ Allow wait time when you ask students to explain their answers.

✪ Teach students how to draw conclusions.

✪ Show students how to organize their written explanations so they make sense.

✪ Have students write down the solution process step-by-step as they work through a problem.

✪ Allow time for discussion of the solution process and have students explain how they solved the problem. Compare the different methods, if applicable.

✪ Provide opportunities for students to evaluate—listen, analyze, and respond to—the mathematical thinking of others.

Math Language Connections (cont.)
Cracking the Code: Word Problems (cont.)

Areas of Difficulty

The following components—reading, thinking, solving, and explaining—are the most troublesome for ELLs. Be aware of these areas of difficulty and consider addressing some of them with your students. Doing so will create a more open, honest, and productive math environment.

Reading Skills	Thinking Skills
Students often . . . • read too quickly. • read below grade level. • skip unknown vocabulary. • do not identify known and unknown factors in a problem. • do not notice key facts and information. • do not read the entire problem.	Students often . . . • do not think through the problem. • subtract or divide larger numbers. • guess. • apply the most recent skill they learned, even if it is irrelevant. • do not break a problem down into its parts. • give up too easily.
Solution Process	**Explain the Answer**
Students often . . . • make computation errors. • do not understand which operation to use. • use an incorrect procedure. • work too carelessly or too fast. • jump to conclusions partway through the problem. • guess at an answer. • solve only part of a multi-step problem. • attempt only one solution process and then give up.	Students often . . . • leave out one or more steps. • do not show evidence of their work. • do not answer the question the problem is asking. • do not use math words correctly. • do not include labels. • write in incomplete sentences. • do not state their thoughts clearly.

Students often think that . . .
- every problem presented by the teacher or in a textbook makes sense and can be solved.
- there is only one correct numerical answer to every word problem.
- they should add, subtract, multiply, or divide all the numbers given in the problem.

Math Language Connections *(cont.)*
Cracking the Code: Word Problems *(cont.)*

Understanding Keywords

Word problems are challenging because they need to be simplified and converted into equations in order to be solved. Familiarize your students with operation-specific terminology, such as what is listed below. Doing so will help your students decode word problems.

Addition	Subtraction
add	decrease (by)
all together	difference
both	fewer
combine	left
in all	less than
increase (by)	lost
plus	minus
sum	more than
total	reduce
	remain
	remainder
	subtract
	take away

Multiplication	Division
multiply	average
product	cut
times	divide (evenly)
twice	equal pieces/parts/groups
	half
	quotient
	ratio
	shared
	split

Math Language Connections (cont.)
Cracking the Code: Word Problems (cont.)

Sample Word Problem

Discuss as a class how to solve the following sample problem. Focus more on communicating about how to solve the problem rather than on finding the answer. Consider asking the questions below to model the problem-solving process.

> The fifth-graders are going to visit their first-grade buddies. There are 26 fifth-graders. They are taking a bag of animal crackers to share with the first-grade class. There are 365 animal crackers in the bag. The first-grade class has 22 students.
>
> **1.** If only the first-graders are given the animal crackers, how many will each receive? *(16, with 13 crackers left over)*
>
> **2.** How many animal crackers will each student receive if all the fifth-graders have animal crackers, too?
> *(7 crackers, with 29 crackers left over)*

✪ What strategies can we use to think about this problem? *(equal groups, counting by 2s or 4s, estimation, drawing pictures, writing equations)*

✪ Which word(s) can we highlight to help us understand the structure of this problem? *(each)*

✪ How can we determine each first-grader's equal share? *(Divide the total number of crackers by the number of students or count by 2s or 4s to distribute crackers in a drawing.)*

✪ How can we use estimation to help us think about this problem? *(Estimate how many times 22 goes into 365 by rounding numbers.)*

✪ How many crackers do you estimate each child will receive? *(15)*

✪ Which operation(s) will we use to make sure that each child receives the same amount? *(multiplication or division)*

✪ What does it mean to "multiply"? *(To "multiply" means to figure out how many crackers are used in all; 22 students each receive 10 crackers. How many crackers have I used so far?)* What does it mean to "divide"? *(To "divide" means to separate the total number of crackers into equal piles for each student.)*

✪ How many animal crackers will be left over? *(13 for first-graders, 29 if all students have crackers)*

✪ How will we know if our answer makes sense? *(We can multiply the number of crackers each child has by the number of children to find out how many crackers we used; we will have to add back in any leftover crackers to arrive at the total amount from the beginning.)*

Math Language Connections *(cont.)*
Cracking the Code: Word Problems *(cont.)*

Steps to Solving Word Problems

Discuss the following problem-solving steps to help your students think about how to solve word problems. Encourage students to compare different problem-solving strategies and to create a checklist for classroom display.

Use the sample charts below as guides. The first one can be used when modeling a problem for the class. The second one can be used when students solve problems independently.

Model for the Class

1. Display the problem for the class.

2. Read the problem aloud and express questions or uncertainties.

3. Think aloud about any word meanings needed to understand the problem.

4. Re-read the problem.

5. Restate the problem in your own words.

6. Summarize what the question is asking.

7. Plan which operations and problem-solving strategies you will use to solve the problem.

8. Have students check your work.

Have Students Work Independently

1. Read the problem.

2. Interpret the language and math references to understand what the problem is asking.

3. Analyze the problem to determine its structure.

4. Choose a solution process.

5. Solve the problem.

6. Show your work.

7. Explain your answer orally and/or in writing.

Math Language Connections *(cont.)*
Math Literacy

Literacy instruction in math class helps students learn to read and write about math. Students need good reading comprehension skills for reading math texts, directions, and word problems. Consider incorporating the following reading and writing tips into your math curriculum.

Tips for Incorporating Reading and Writing Into Math Curriculum

- ✪ Preview the math material(s) as necessary to generate interest in the topic and to help students access their background knowledge.

- ✪ Show students the meanings of math symbols.

- ✪ Show students how to distinguish between the main idea and details in math problems; often the main idea will be at the end of a problem.

- ✪ Provide graphic organizers or outlines (pg. 44) to help students make sense out of text. Then model how to use these organizers.

- ✪ Provide explanations as necessary to help students see the progression of steps in a math problem-solving process. (Content-specific text may make assumptions about readers' underlying knowledge.)

- ✪ Demonstrate and teach students how to think aloud (pg. 59) to help them understand math texts.

- ✪ Provide books about math topics and have students read and talk about their reading to increase their comprehension of math concepts and vocabulary.

- ✪ Encourage students to use correct math vocabulary when they write about math by having them refer to classroom resources such as word walls, vocabulary charts or posters, student reference cards, or glossaries and dictionaries.

- ✪ Introduce a variety of texts (e.g., textbooks, fiction stories, biographies of mathematicians) to help students become familiar with math concepts.

- ✪ Consider the reading level of instructional materials. Make sure your materials are developmentally appropriate.

- ✪ Demonstrate how mathematical reading requires students to read data left to right, right to left (number lines), top to bottom (tables), and diagonally (graphs).

- ✪ Have students ask themselves the following questions as they read:
    - ★ Why do I need to know this?
    - ★ How can I use this information?
    - ★ What is most interesting to me about this information?
    - ★ How does this relate to something else I've learned?

- ✪ Have students use writing to organize, clarify, reflect on, and explore their math ideas.

- ✪ Have students evaluate and discuss their own writing, as well as that of their classmates.

- ✪ Use math journals (pg. 49) to encourage struggling students to express questions and difficulties. Provide feedback in the form of personal written responses or one-on-one conferences.

- ✪ Use students' writing to informally assess their understanding of math vocabulary and concepts. Check student writing for fluency.

Math Language Connections (cont.)

Math Literacy (cont.)

Math Writing Activities

- ❂ Have students rewrite problems in their own words. Instruct students to describe their step-by-step plans for solving the problems and then finding the solutions. Encourage students to analyze how well their strategies worked to solve the problems.

- ❂ Have students write math problems using the skills they learned in class. Consider the following sample prompts:

  - ★ Write an addition problem that has an answer of 4,652.

  - ★ Write a math problem to go with a displayed picture.

  - ★ Write a story problem that involves multiplication and subtraction of decimals.

  - ★ Write and illustrate a story problem for a student in a lower grade.

  - ★ Write a step-by-step explanation of how to solve an equation or how to graph data for a student who was absent.

- ❂ Have students write a "how to" piece for another student that explains how they solved a particular problem.

- ❂ Model how to identify errors in solving a math problem. Guide students to understanding what types of errors they might make in arriving at an incorrect solution. Have students practice explaining their errors, first verbally and then in writing.

- ❂ Ask students to write math essays about a particular concept. Suggest that students compare and contrast multiplication and division of fractions, for example, or characteristics of lines. Students may choose to include their own ideas and feelings about learning a new math concept and what connections they make between the new information and math they already know.

- ❂ Provide opportunities for students to develop a correspondence relationship with a math pen pal. Have students use a simple method, such as a dialogue journal, to write to a classmate or a student in another class, grade, and/or school. If desired, integrate technology (e.g., emails, messaging).

- ❂ Have students create cartoons with dialogue to explain math concepts.

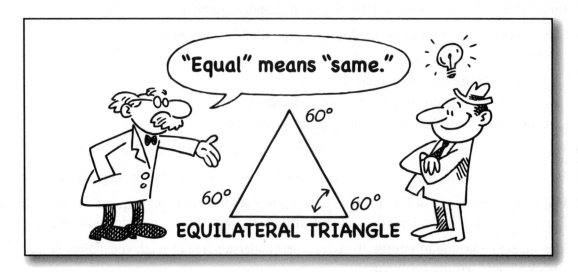

Practical Classroom Applications
Sample Lesson: Think Like a Mathematician

Objective

Given a role-playing scenario, students will approach the problem from either a mathematician's perspective or a non-mathematician's perspective and compare the two approaches to problem solving.

Vocabulary

mathematician: a person who is an expert (someone who specializes) in mathematics

Materials

- ✪ "Isacco the Mathematician" (pg. 85), one copy for class display and one copy per student (optional)

- ✪ "Marius the Non-Mathematician" (pg. 86), one copy for class display and one copy per student (optional)

Preparation

Prepare "Isacco the Mathematician" and "Marius the Non-Mathematician" for display using chart paper, an overhead projector, or an interactive whiteboard.

Opening

1. Write the word *mathematician* in the center circle of a web graphic organizer. Read the word aloud and ask students to share their thoughts about what the word means, the type of person it describes, what such a person might do, etc.

2. Clarify student thinking as necessary with a formal definition of *mathematician*.

Directions, Part I

1. Display "Isacco the Mathematician" and "Marius the Non-Mathematician."

2. Have students read about Isacco and discuss the characteristics of a mathematician. Point out that Marius is not a mathematician and, therefore, has different thoughts and characteristics. Discuss some of the thoughts he might have. Write them in the thought bubbles.

3. Compare and contrast how Isacco and his friend, Marius, might approach a task—for example, setting up a video-game system or reading a map when taking a trip.

Practical Classroom Applications *(cont.)*
Sample Lesson: Think Like a Mathematician *(cont.)*

Directions, Part II

1. Pose questions, such as the following:

   ★ Isacco and Marius each want to purchase and set up a video-game system. How will each of them decide what to buy?

   Possible answer for Isacco: A mathematician would choose a system based on specific factors, such as desired features, convenience (handheld vs. console unit), game availability, and cost. Isacco might create a diagram to illustrate the costs and specifications of various systems.

   ★ How will they learn how to use the video-game system?

   Possible answer for Isacco: Sometimes mathematicians need help to solve problems; when they set up a game system or a new game, they might ask someone for help understanding the manual.

   ★ How can Isacco use his experience with numbers, symbols, and math ideas to think about the problem?

   Possible answer: Mathematicians know that they can solve problems by thinking about similar problems they have solved before. They might try (e.g., rent, borrow) a game first before buying it. When learning how to play a new game, they would think about other games they have played before.

2. Divide the class into two or more groups. Assign each group a position of mathematician (Isacco) or non-mathematician (Marius) and have them explain how they would approach and solve the problem from that person's perspective.

Closing

Have each group present its perspective, including how they would approach and solve the problem and why this approach would or would not be effective.

Extension

Have students use what they have learned about thinking like a mathematician to write directions for someone else, telling him or her how to play a specific game, make a wise purchase decision, etc.

Interactive Whiteboard Options

✪ Have students contribute directly to the web for class discussion during the opening activity.

✪ Take notes as student groups present their perspectives in a class discussion to review how to think like a mathematician.

Isacco the Mathematician

Marius the Non-Mathematician

Practical Classroom Applications *(cont.)*
Sample Lesson: Meta-Cognitive Thinking

Objective
Students will become aware of their thinking processes in math.

Vocabulary

meta-cognitive: understanding how one thinks, knows, or learns something

operation: a math process, such as addition, subtraction, multiplication, and division (+, −, x, and ÷)

organize: to put in order

Materials

- ❂ "Thinking Questions" (pg. 89), enough copies for each student to have two questions
- ❂ hat or other container

Preparation

1. Photocopy "Thinking Questions" and "Sentence Stems for Additional Support" (pg. 89), and cut the questions into strips.

2. Place the questions into the "thinking cap" (hat or other container).

Opening

1. Help students think about their math experiences by having them turn and talk with partners about what they did in a recent math lesson.

2. Remind students to have a plan when solving math problems: (1) Think about the problem; (2) Use arithmetic operations; (3) Remember how to solve similar problems.

3. Inroduce new math term/concept: meta-cognitive thinking.

Directions, Part I

1. Teach students the five steps of meta-cognitive thinking:

   ⋆ Plan and prepare for new learning by asking the following questions:

   - What will I learn?

   - How will I learn it?

   ⋆ Choose a teaching strategy (pp. 38–62) and organize thinking by asking the following questions:

   - What do I do if I read a word I don't understand?

   - How do I figure out what to do to solve a problem?

Directions, Part I *(cont.)*

* ★ Manage and use the chosen strategy by asking the following questions:

    * Are the things I'm doing helping me to solve the problem?

    * Do I understand what I'm doing?

    * Does this new math concept make sense?

    * How is this like another problem I have solved?

* ★ Monitor the effectiveness of the strategy by asking the following questions:

    * What can I do if my first strategy doesn't work?

    * What other steps can I take to try to solve this problem?

* ★ Evaluate new learning by asking the following questions:

    * What questions do I still have?

    * How well did my strategies work to solve the problem?

    * Did I learn what I set out to learn?

2. Display or distribute a sample math problem or challenge.

3. Divide the class into five groups. Assign each group one step to consider as they think about how they would solve the problem. Emphasize that students will not solve the problem, they will just think about how they would solve the problem.

Directions, Part II

1. Have each student take two slips of paper from the "thinking cap."

2. Ask students to think and write their responses to the questions on their slips of paper.

3. If desired, use the sentence stems to help ELLs answer questions about thinking.

Closing

Create a class poster with an outline of a person in the center and several thinking bubbles around the person. Have students share the responses they wrote in Part II. Add the responses to the class poster.

Extension

Have students extend their learning about meta-cognitive thinking by applying the questions to a math challenge or math-related project. Students might record their thinking, explaining their problem-solving processes for display in a math exhibit.

Interactive Whiteboard Option

As students share their responses to the questions, have them write them on a class notes page. Save and print the page for all students to use as a reference when they are problem solving.

Practical Classroom Applications *(cont.)*
Sample Lesson: Meta-Cognitive Thinking *(cont.)*

Thinking Questions

What do I do to get ready to learn a new math concept?

What did I think about _____ ?

What new thing did I learn when I thought about _____?

What plan of action will I take to solve this problem?

How will I remember what to do when I see this kind of problem in the future?

What tools will I use to solve this problem?

What do I do when I don't know what to do next?

How do I check my work to make sure my solution is correct?

What does this part of the (graph, equation, etc.) represent?

What does this part of the problem ask me to do?

What do I need to do next?

What symbols do I need to use in this problem?

What does this word mean?

How did I get these numbers? Do they make sense?

What do I notice from the data?

How can I organize my information?

Sentence Stems for Additional Support

- I solved a problem once by _____.
- I know how to _____ in math.
- When I need to solve a problem, the first thing I do is _____.
- I organize my thinking about a problem by _____.
- Because I understand _____, I can _____.

Practical Classroom Applications (cont.)
Sample Lesson: Coordinate Planes

Objective

Given a sample story, students will learn the context of vocabulary related to coordinate planes and create simple coordinate planes.

Vocabulary

coordinate plane: the plane containing the x-axis and the y-axis

coordinates: a set of numbers used to show the position of a point on a plane

distance: the amount of space between two places; the length of a line between two points

grid: a pattern of horizontal and vertical lines spaced out evenly

intersect: to meet or cross something; intersecting lines meet or cross each other.

locate: to find

negative number: a number less than zero

ordered pair: a pair of numbers that shows the position of a point on a coordinate grid

point: an exact location; it shows position but not size.

positive number: a number greater than zero

scale: the relationship between distances on maps and actual distances; a machine used to weigh people or objects

vertical: upright, or straight up and down

x-axis: the line on a graph that runs horizontally (side-to-side) through zero

y-axis: the line on a graph that runs vertically (straight up and down) through zero

Materials

- ❂ "Find It!—Word List" and "Find It!—Story" (pg. 92), one copy for class display
- ❂ "The Map—Word List" (pg. 93), halve each copy, one half for class display and one half per student
- ❂ "The Map—Story" (pg. 94), one copy for class display and one copy per student
- ❂ plain graph or grid paper (optional for closing activity)

Preparation

Prepare the sample story for classroom display—cover the story part and show only the word list.

Opening

1. Explain the concept behind a Mad Libs-type story.

2. Display "Find It!—Word List." As a class, choose math words that match the description provided (e.g. verb, noun).

3. Reveal the "Find It!—Story" part of the page. Substitute the words missing from the story with the words the students have chosen.

4. Read the complete story aloud. Then discuss which words would have been more appropriate for each space. (Possible answers are provided at the bottom of the page.)

Practical Classroom Applications *(cont.)*
Sample Lesson: Coordinate Planes *(cont.)*

Directions

1. Give each student a copy of "The Map—Word List." Display a copy on a chart, an overhead projector, or an interactive whiteboard.

2. As a class, choose math words that match the description provided (e.g., verb, noun, adjective). Record the responses for the class.

3. Now give each student a copy of "The Map—Story." Display a copy on a chart, an overhead projector, or an interactive whiteboard.

4. Have students take turns substituting the words missing from the story with the words they had already chosen.

5. Read through the story together as a class. Assure ELLs that the story may not make sense.

6. Discuss as a class which math words could be used in each blank to create a story that does make sense.

7. Display a copy of "The Map—Story Answer Key" on a chart, an overhead projector, or an interactive whiteboard. Review the answers, as well as their meanings.

Closing

1. Have students draw simple coordinate planes and mark specific points of items in the classroom. As a class, determine an appropriate scale, such as 1 inch = 1 foot.

2. Invite students to use a classmate's coordinate grid to find specific items in the classroom.

Extension

1. Have students create math stories and word lists for partners to solve. Encourage students to refer to word walls, vocabulary charts, a math book, or other vocabulary reference materials for ideas.

2. Students will trade with partners and complete their partners' story word lists. Then they will reveal the stories and fill in the blanks.

3. Invite students to share completed stories with the class as time allows.

Interactive Whiteboard Option

Use a word-processing program on the interactive whiteboard to have the class work together to create a math story and word list. Share the word list and story with another class, if desired.

Practical Classroom Applications (cont.)
Sample Lesson: Coordinate Planes (cont.)

Find It!—Word List

1. _____ (noun)

2. _____ (noun)

3. _____ (plural noun)

4. _____ (verb, past tense)

5. _____ (plural noun)

6. _____ (plural noun)

7. _____ (plural noun)

Find It!—Story

Josh and Elijah drew a _____ [1] of their

neighborhood. They drew a vertical _____ [2]

on the left side of the map. They wrote _____ [3]

next to the line. Josh wrote numbers across the bottom of

the map. Elijah _____ [4] the map into

_____ [5]. They used the numbers

and lines to help them locate _____ [6],

_____ [7], and other landmarks near their

houses.

Answers: (1) map, (2) line, (3) numbers, (4) divided, (5) squares, (6) trees, (7) stores

The Map—Word List

1. _____ (noun)
2. _____ (adjective)
3. _____ (plural noun)
4. _____ (adjective)
5. _____ (noun)
6. _____ (noun)
7. _____ (adjective)
8. _____ (adjective)
9. _____ (adjective)
10. _____ (verb, present tense)
11. _____ (verb, present tense)
12. _____ (noun)
13. _____ (noun)
14. _____ (verb, past tense)
15. _____ (adjective)

The Map—Word List

1. _____ (noun)
2. _____ (adjective)
3. _____ (plural noun)
4. _____ (adjective)
5. _____ (noun)
6. _____ (noun)
7. _____ (adjective)
8. _____ (adjective)
9. _____ (adjective)
10. _____ (verb, present tense)
11. _____ (verb, present tense)
12. _____ (noun)
13. _____ (noun)
14. _____ (verb, past tense)
15. _____ (adjective)

The Map—Story

Justin could hardly wait. Tonight his family would have dinner at his uncle's house. Justin always enjoyed spending time with his uncle and playing in the oversized backyard.

"Hi, guys! We're having my favorite dinner: barbecued hamburgers," Uncle Bryon greeted them.

"It's my favorite dinner, too," Justin said.

"I have a surprise for you after dinner." Justin's uncle worked as a math teacher at the high school, and he liked to explain new ideas to Justin. After dinner Uncle Bryon handed Justin a piece of paper. It was a _____ [1] with symbols in various squares of the grid. Justin noticed several numbers in the lower corner of the page.

"This looks like a _____ [2] map," Justin said. "I notice the map has _____, [3] but why does it have all these numbers?" Justin pointed to the outside lines of the grid. "Why are some lines on the grid darker than others?"

"This kind of 'map' is called a _____ [4] _____ [5]," Uncle Bryon said. "Do you remember how to locate a _____ [6] from math last year? Let's practice. At what point is the tree located?"

Justin looked at the coordinate plane. "I think it's at three, but there aren't any letters to go with it. Some of these numbers have a minus sign, but I don't understand why."

Uncle Bryon tried to explain. "The numbers along the bottom of the grid form a number line. Numbers to the left of zero are _____ [7]; numbers to the right are _____ [8]. This is the x-axis. Instead of letters on the other side, you see a _____ [9] number line, the y-axis. You can still _____ [10] a point on the grid by finding where two lines intersect. The tree is where the line labeled four _____ [11] with the line labeled three. Its location is called (4,3). Those two numbers form an ordered pair."

"How will this help me find the treasure? Your yard doesn't have lines and numbers."

Uncle Bryon laughed. "You're right. Look at the _____ [12] at the bottom of the page. It says that one square equals one meter. You can pretend my yard has lines drawn on it. Use the map to figure out the _____ [13] from one point to the next."

"Is there really a treasure _____ [14] at the coordinate marked '**X**'?"

"You'll have to discover that for yourself. If you find the _____ [15] coordinate and you need a particular tool, let me know."

"Thanks," Justin said, as he headed toward the backyard. "I'm sure I'll remember what I've learned about coordinate planes after this adventure!"

The Map—Story Answer Key

Justin could hardly wait. Tonight his family would have dinner at his uncle's house. Justin always enjoyed spending time with his uncle and playing in the oversized backyard.

"Hi, guys! We're having my favorite dinner: barbecued hamburgers," Uncle Bryon greeted them.

"It's my favorite dinner, too," Justin said.

"I have a surprise for you after dinner." Justin's uncle worked as a math teacher at the high school, and he liked to explain new ideas to Justin. After dinner Uncle Bryon handed Justin a piece of paper. It was a <u>grid</u> [1] with symbols in various squares of the grid. Justin noticed several numbers in the lower corner of the page.

"This looks like a <u>treasure</u> [2] map," Justin said. "I notice the map has <u>symbols,</u> [3] but why does it have all these numbers?" Justin pointed to the outside lines of the grid. "Why are some lines on the grid darker than others?"

"This kind of 'map' is called a <u>coordinate</u> [4] <u>plane</u> [5]," Uncle Bryon said. "Do you remember how to locate a <u>point</u> [6] from math last year? Let's practice. At what point is the tree located?"

Justin looked at the coordinate plane. "I think it's at three, but there aren't any letters to go with it. Some of these numbers have a minus sign, but I don't understand why."

Uncle Bryon tried to explain. "The numbers along the bottom of the grid form a number line. Numbers to the left of zero are <u>negative</u> [7]; numbers to the right are <u>positive</u> [8]. This is the x-axis. Instead of letters on the other side, you see a <u>vertical</u> [9] number line, the y-axis. You can still <u>locate</u> [10] a point on the grid by finding where two lines intersect. The tree is where the line labeled four <u>intersects</u> [11] with the line labeled three. Its location is called (4,3). Those two numbers form an ordered pair."

"How will this help me find the treasure? Your yard doesn't have lines and numbers."

Uncle Bryon laughed. "You're right. Look at the <u>scale</u> [12] at the bottom of the page. It says that one square equals one meter. You can pretend my yard has lines drawn on it. Use the map to figure out the <u>distance</u> [13] from one point to the next."

"Is there really a treasure <u>buried</u> [14] at the coordinate marked '**X**'?"

"You'll have to discover that for yourself. If you find the <u>matching</u> [15] coordinate and you need a particular tool, let me know."

"Thanks," Justin said, as he headed toward the backyard. "I'm sure I'll remember what I've learned about coordinate planes after this adventure!"

Practical Classroom Applications (cont.)
Sample Lesson: Fractions and Decimals

Objective
Given a review of decimals, students will work in small groups to practice solving problems and receive help from classmates.

Vocabulary

decimal point: a dot used to separate a whole number and a fractional part of a whole number

fraction: a part of a whole number

hundredth: one part of something that has been divided into 100 equal parts; it is written as $\frac{1}{100}$ or 0.01.

tenth: one part of something that has been divided into 10 equal parts; it is written as $\frac{1}{10}$ or 0.1.

thousandth: one part of something that has been divided into 1,000 equal parts; it is written as $\frac{1}{1000}$ or 0.001.

Materials

- ✪ place value charts, 100s grids, base-10 blocks, Unifix cubes, Cuisenaire rods, number cards, or other graphic representations for fractions and decimals
- ✪ sample problems with fractions, decimals, and percent (see examples, pg. 97)

Opening

1. Review place value for decimals using drawings (number lines, boxes, fraction bars, or 100s grids), physical models (cubes, rods, number cards), or other graphic representations.

2. Remind students that the decimal point can be read; do this while reading a decimal number.

3. Teach students to write a "zero" to the left of the decimal point to indicate a decimal fraction with a value of less than one.

4. Review the relationship between fractions and decimals and how a fractional number can be written as a fraction or a decimal.

5. Make sure students understand each place value (tenths, hundredths, and thousandths, respectively) before introducing the next place in decimal notation.

Directions

1. Divide students into mixed-ability groups of three to five students each. Have groups work with one or more problems that give them practice working with fractions.

2. Encourage students to use drawings, physical models, or other graphic representations to problem solve and check for understanding.

3. Monitor groups closely as they work. As soon as one group understands the concept, have each student in that group move to a different group and help the other groups in the classroom understand the concept.

Practical Classroom Applications *(cont.)*
Sample Lesson: Fractions and Decimals *(cont.)*

Directions *(cont.)*

4. As time allows, restructure groups again and have students work one or more problems using decimals.

5. Monitor groups closely and send students from the first group that demonstrates comprehension to help other groups in the class.

Closing

Work together as a class to create a graphic organizer that explains how fractions and decimals relate to each other.

Extension

Divide students into groups. Have each group write a word problem with fractions or decimals. Encourage them to write about real-life topics, including racecar times, student times in running races, distance around a track (tenths of a mile or fractional parts), measurements (U.S. customary and metric units).

Interactive Whiteboard Option

Students can drag decimal or fractional numbers to place them in the correct order.

Sample Problems

1. There are 70 students in the school band. One-fifth of the students play clarinet. How many students play clarinet? *(14 students)*

2. Hunter and Taylor agreed to meet at the library. They each walked to the library from where they lived. Together it took them $18 \frac{3}{4}$ minutes. It took Taylor twice as much time as it took Hunter. How many minutes did it take each of them to walk to the library? *(Hunter—$6 \frac{1}{4}$ minutes; Taylor—$12 \frac{1}{2}$ minutes)*

3. Juan is making cookies. The recipe has $\frac{1}{4}$ cup of walnuts and $\frac{1}{3}$ cup of almonds. How many nuts does Juan need in all? *($\frac{7}{12}$ cup of nuts)*

4. Ryan earned $50.00 mowing lawns over the summer. He put $40.00 in savings. He then received 50% of what he has in savings from his grandmother for his birthday. How much money does he have in his savings now? *(Ryan had $40.00 in savings. Then he received $\frac{1}{2}$ of $40.00 from his grandmother [$20.00]. $40.00 + $20.00 = $60.00 in savings)*

Practical Classroom Applications *(cont.)*
Sample Lesson: Geometry Notes

Objective
Given a sample, students will learn how to take notes in math class.

Vocabulary

closed figure: a shape that begins and ends at the same point

figure: a shape; a written number; an amount given in numbers

open figure: a shape that is not completely closed; it does not begin and end at the same point.

plane figure/shape: a two-dimensional shape; it has width and length but no depth.

solid figure: a three-dimensional shape

Materials

- ✪ "Sample Cornell Notes" (pg. 100), one copy for class display and one copy per student
- ✪ "Cornell Notes Form" (pg. 101), one copy for class display and one copy per student

Opening

1. Introduce the concept of taking notes (pg. 30). Explain that when students take notes, they make connections between what they already know and new concepts they learn. Writing down information also helps us to remember what we hear.

2. Introduce the concept of Cornell notes as one method to take notes. Students use a two-column format to list main ideas and details. In math class, the left column includes main points, concepts, and keywords, while the right column includes simple definitions and examples. Additional questions, thoughts, and summaries are noted in the bottom half of the page. (*Note:* Students might prefer to fill in the top half of the page and then use their notes to generate questions that will help them remember what was heard or read.)

Directions

1. Give each student a copy of the "Sample Cornell Notes" and "Cornell Notes Form." Model how to take notes, using the following steps:

   ★ Discuss step-by-step how to take notes using the sample.

   ★ Focus students' attention on the "Cornell Notes Form."

   ★ Present a goal or objective for the lesson.

   ★ Present information in a logical sequence.

   ★ Guide students to write down key information by writing it on the board, including it in a presentation, or giving students some other visual cue.

   ★ Show students how to use graphics in their notes, such as stars, arrows, brackets, etc.

   ★ If desired, use any other note-taking format you have developed that might work well for your students.

Directions *(cont.)*

2. Use interactive techniques, such as the following:

   ★ Turn and share with partners for one minute.

   ★ Write examples or questions on individual whiteboards.

   ★ Ask questions to stump the teacher.

   ★ Participate in partner or team competitions.

3. Provide a word bank or sentence frames as needed to help ELLs follow along when taking notes.

Closing

1. Have students trade their papers with partners and read their partners' notes.

2. Ask students to write one or two things they learned from reading their partners' notes.

3. If time permits, have students write reflective journal entries or encouraging notes to their partners.

Extension

Provide students with an opportunity to use their notes. For example, students may enjoy identifying geometric figures on the playground. Invite students to design their own playgrounds using various geometric figures, and have them explain why their designs would be effective.

Interactive Whiteboard Option

Display the sample note-taking form and have volunteers contribute to a sheet of class notes for a specific part of the content.

Sample Cornell Notes

Name: Archie Euclid	Date: 10/01
Topic: Geometric Figures	**Class:** Math

Main points, concepts, and keywords:
 	
Types of figures:
 	
  Plane
   • square, circle, triangle
 	
  Closed
   • square, circle, triangle
 	
  Open
   • parabola, hyperbola
 	
  Solid
   • cube, sphere, pyramid
	Definitions and examples:
	
	a two-dimensional shape
	
	a shape that begins and ends at the same point
	
	a shape that doesn't begin and end at the same point; it is not completely closed.
	
	a three-dimensional shape

Questions: What is the difference between a closed figure and an open figure? What is the difference between a plane shape and a solid figure? What are some real-life examples of plane shapes? What are some real-life examples of solid figures?	With closed figures, you can go around the edge and get back where you started because the beginning and end point is the same. A plane shape is two-dimensional (flat like a piece of paper), while a solid figure is three-dimensional (has depth, like a box). checkerboard (square), dime (circle), yield sign (triangle) box of tissues (cube), ball (sphere), ice-cream cone (cone)

Summary:
Geometric figures can either be plane (two-dimensional) or solid (three-dimensional). Of the plane variety, they can either be closed or open (shapes do or do not begin and end at the same point).

There are many examples of plane shapes, including squares, circles, and triangles. Some real-life examples are checkerboards, dimes, and yield signs. There are also many examples of solid figures, which include cubes, spheres, and cones. Some real-life examples are tissue boxes, balls, and ice-cream cones.

Practical Classroom Applications *(cont.)*
Sample Lesson: Geometry Notes *(cont.)*

Cornell Notes Form

Name:	Date:
Topic:	Class:

Main points, concepts, and keywords:	Definitions and examples:

Questions:	

Summary:

Practical Classroom Applications *(cont.)*
Sample Lesson: Motion Geometry

Objective

Given vocabulary and a demonstration, students will use motion geometry to create squares from shape pieces.

Vocabulary

flip: a type of symmetry where one half is the mirror image of the other half; it's also called "reflection."

reflection: a type of symmetry where one half is the mirror image of the other half; it's also called "flip."

rotation: to move a figure around a given point; it's also called "turn."

slide: to move a figure without flipping or turning it; the figure looks the same but is in a different place; it's also called "translation."

symmetry: a balanced arrangement of parts on either side of a line or around a central point

transformation: moving a shape so that it is in a different position but still has the same size, area, angles, and line lengths

translation: to move a figure without flipping or turning it; the figure looks the same but is in a different place; it's also called "slide."

trapezoid: a shape that has four straight sides; only one pair of opposite sides is parallel.

turn: to move a figure around a given point; it's also called "rotation."

Materials

- ✪ "Shapes Within Shapes" (pg. 104), one copy for display
- ✪ pattern blocks, tangrams, or opaque plastic shapes for overhead projector
- ✪ "Tangram Pieces" (pg. 104), four sets per student or group
- ✪ envelopes, one per student or group
- ✪ tape or glue for each student or group
- ✪ plain white paper, one piece per student or group
- ✪ colored pencils (optional)

Preparation

1. Photocopy "Tangram Pieces" onto heavy paper or cardstock enough times so that each student or group can receive a set of four.

2. Cut the pieces apart and place four sets into each envelope.

Opening

1. Display Figure A from "Shapes Within Shapes" on chart paper, an overhead projector, or an interactive whiteboard. Conceal Figure B.
    - ★ Ask students what shapes they see within the larger shape *(triangles)*. Have students count the number of individual shapes.

Practical Classroom Applications *(cont.)*
Sample Lesson: Motion Geometry *(cont.)*

Opening *(cont.)*

2. Now display Figure B and discuss the shapes students notice within this shape.
   * Ask students how shapes can be flipped (reflected) to create new shapes.
     (The two outer triangles can be flipped and turned to create a pentagon.)

3. Introduce or review the vocabulary to describe motion geometry: turns (rotations), flips (reflections), and slides (translations). Demonstrate each motion with pattern blocks, tangrams, or opaque plastic shapes on the overhead projector.

4. Write each word on the board and point to the word while demonstrating the related motion. Have students repeat each word as volunteers take turns performing the movements.

5. Explain that a transformation of a shape or figure can incorporate any of these movements.
   * Ask students which movement symmetry most closely represents *(reflection)*.

Directions

1. Have students work individually, with partners, or in small groups depending on students' experiences and abilities with motion geometry. Distribute prepared "Tangram Pieces" envelopes.

2. Ask students to assemble the pieces to make four squares. Students should use all the pieces provided when making the four squares with no pieces left over. So if one set contains 1 square, 3 triangles, and 1 trapezoid, students should use all those pieces to make one square. Because there are four sets in each envelope, students will have four (large) squares. Remind students to reflect (flip), rotate (turn), and translate (slide) pieces, as necessary.

Closing

1. Have students tape or glue one of their completed squares to a single sheet of paper.

2. Ask students to label each of the smaller shapes that make up the square. If desired, have students color each shape a different color to help them distinguish between the shapes.

3. Write the words of various shapes on the board as needed to help students write the names of shapes.

Extension

1. Ask students which larger shapes in the classroom can be divided into smaller shapes.

2. Have students draw and label the shapes they see.

3. If desired, have students measure the shapes to find the perimeter or area.

Interactive Whiteboard Option

Use shapes in a flip chart and have students practice transformational movements with the shapes.

Practical Classroom Applications (cont.)
Sample Lesson: Motion Geometry (cont.)

Shapes Within Shapes

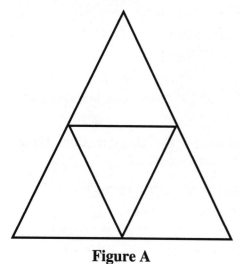

Figure A

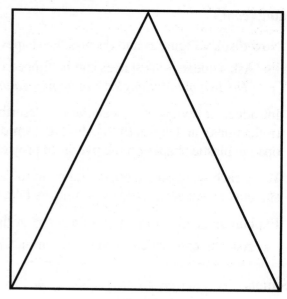

Figure B

Tangram Pieces

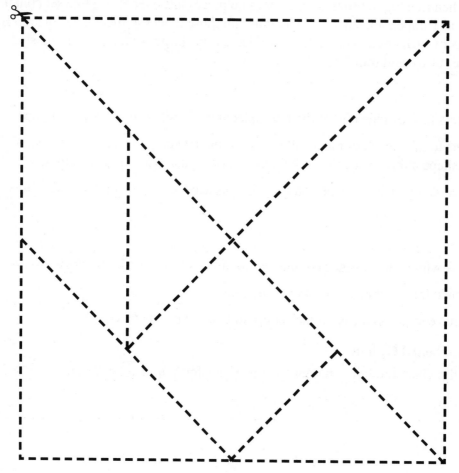

Practical Classroom Applications *(cont.)*
Assessments and Rubrics

Teachers assess student work to determine how well students have learned new math concepts. In math, it is particularly important for students to understand one concept before moving on to the next, since math tends to build upon a foundation. Students can demonstrate their learning in a variety of ways: by completing in-class and homework assignments, by performing a process or series of actions to demonstrate understanding, or by taking a test.

When planning assessments, be aware of your students'. . .

- language proficiency levels.
- cultural backgrounds.
- educational backgrounds.

- learning styles.
- individual goals and needs.
- progress and growth over time.

Use a variety of procedures and techniques to assess students, such as the following:

✪ Formative assessments (e.g., class discussions, student portfolios, math journals)—to make adjustments in teaching and to help students identify changes they need to make in their learning

✪ Summative assessments (e.g., quizzes or tests after a unit of study)—to check comprehension of material studied and realize what requires reviewing

✪ Student portfolios—to demonstrate student growth and learning in math; include formative and summative assessments

✪ Rubrics—to assess student math assignments or math journals

★ Sample Activity: Have students solve a problem and write a description of the steps they took to solve the problem. Distribute copies of a rubric, such as the one below, and have students trade papers to evaluate their classmates' problem-solving processes. Allow time for students to discuss how they scored their partners' papers and to revise their writing as needed for clarification.

Sample Rubric

	1	2	3	4
Includes all the steps necessary to solve the problem				
Steps are explained in a logical order				
Explanation includes what the student did and why				
Writing is easy to understand				
Drawings include clear labels that are easy to understand				

Connect homework to assessments using the following tips:

- ✪ Make sure homework has a purpose (i.e., reviews concepts, provides additional practice, prepares students for assessment).

- ✪ Use predictable formats for homework assignments and assessments.

- ✪ Assign problems for homework that are similar to test problems; include enough so students can have adequate practice and demonstrate mastery of the concept without feeling overwhelmed.

- ✪ As a class, review examples of student work that meet assessment or rubric guidelines so students can see effective problem-solving solutions.

Modify assessments using the following tips:

- ✪ Remove irrelevant words or phrases.

- ✪ Make sure wording is culturally appropriate.

- ✪ Incorporate assessment formats with which students are familiar.

- ✪ Read aloud, simplify, clarify, and repeat test instructions and actual test items in English. However, do not simplify language for specific terms that relate directly to the standards or concepts being tested.

- ✪ Call attention to key vocabulary words necessary to understanding the content being assessed.

- ✪ Incorporate appropriate graphics to give students visual support.

- ✪ Offer translation assistance but take care not to alter the intended meaning of the test item.

- ✪ Have a translator clarify test instructions or translate vocabulary that does not directly assess content knowledge.

- ✪ Allow a translator to describe students' oral responses directly onto the test document, if possible.

- ✪ Allow extra time for students to complete assessments.

- ✪ Provide word-to-word dictionaries (that do not include definitions).

Teacher Resources
Websites for Educators

Center for Applied Linguistics (CAL): *http://www.cal.org*

CAL publishes research, teacher education, instructional materials, etc., about language, literacy, math language and literacy, assessment, and culture. For a complete list of their math ELL resources, go to "Search" at the top, right-hand side of the page and type "math."

Classroom Zoom: *http://www.classroomzoom.com*

Classroom Zoom is an online subscription service created by Teacher Created Resources. Subscribers to the service have access to more than 11,000 printable lessons—all searchable by grade and subject. Members can also create custom math worksheets. Additionally, there are more than 1,000 free lessons available to nonmembers.

Dave's ESL Café: *http://www.eslcafe.com*

This site is maintained by its founder, Dave Sperling—a teacher with both ESL and EFL instructional experience. Since 1995, Dave has devoted much time and energy to creating a site dedicated to providing ideas for ESL teachers, as well as support for ELLs. On this site, you can find teacher forums, lesson ideas, and even job boards. For math activities, go to "STUFF FOR TEACHERS," then select "Idea Cookbook," and finally "Math."

EnglishCompanion.com: *http://www.englishcompanion.com/Tools/notemaking.html*

The site founder and author of *Tools for Thought*, Jim Burke, lists and explains over 25 different methods for "notemaking"—which includes everything from Cornell notes to linear arrays.

Everything ESL.net: *http://www.everythingesl.net*

Judie Haynes, an ESL teacher from New Jersey with more than 32 years of experience, is the main contributor to this site, which includes lesson plans, teaching tips, and various resources for ESL teachers. There is also a question-and-answer section where visitors are encouraged to ask questions (to Judie) and give responses. For math materials, go to "Search with Google™" and type "math."

Harcourt School Publishers: *http://www.hbschool.com/glossary/math2/index.html*

This site offers a K–6 multimedia math glossary. The student-friendly definitions include colorful, visual examples.

Math and Literature—Make the Connection: *http://www.elemedu.ccs.k12.nc.us/Task_Analyses/ Math/Fifth%20Grade/Connecting_Literature-Fifth_Grade-Math.htm*

This webpage, which was created by Cumberland County Schools (Fayetteville, NC), charts 50 fifth-grade literature choices that have math connections.

Math Is Fun!: *http://www.mathsisfun.com*

Since 2000, this site has been helping teachers and students with math education. It offers math worksheets, activities, games, and an extensive illustrated math dictionary. The site also covers each branch of math, including numbers, algebra, geometry, data, and measurement.

Math TV: *http://www.mathtv.com*

This membership site offers video explanations for basic math (numbers), algebra, geometry, trigonometry, and calculus problems. Many of the videos include Spanish versions. For each skill, there are a number of sample problems to choose from.

National Clearinghouse for English Language Acquisition and Language Instruction Educational Programs (NCELA): *http://www.ncela.gwu.edu*

This site contains information and resources dedicated to Title III (organized by state), standards and assessments, and grants and funding. It also offers webinars, publications (including NCELA's *AccELLerate*), and a resource library to aid ESL teachers in the classroom. Search for math articles and resources using the search bar in the upper, right-hand corner of the main page.

Reading Rockets: *http://www.readingrockets.org*

Reading Rockets, a project created by WETA, is aimed to inform educators and parents on how to teach children to read, why some children struggle with reading, and how adults can help struggling children. The project includes PBS television programs; online resources, such as podcasts and blogs; and professional development opportunities. Strategies, reading guides, and newsletters can also be found on the site. For articles specific to math, type "math" in the search box at the top, right-hand side of the page.

Teachers First: *http://www.teachersfirst.com*

Helping educators since 1998, Teachers First offers teachers more than 12,000 classroom and professional resources, including rubrics, lesson plans, and tips for working with parents, substitutes, and technology. For math-specific classroom resources, go to "Classroom Resources," select the intended grade level(s), and search "math."

TrackStar: *http://trackstar.4teachers.org*

TrackStar helps you create and store online lessons and activities. These interactive lessons are called Tracks. To make a Track, you simply add annotations and website addresses. Or you can access the hundreds of thousands that have been made by other educators. To find math ELL tracks, click on "Browse by Subject/Grades" under "Find a Track." Next, in the Subject(s) section, select "English as a Second Language" and "Math."

Teacher Resources (cont.)
Translation Websites

Bing Translator: *http://www.microsofttranslator.com*

This free translator can translate over 30 languages. Users have the option of copying and pasting text into a box or entering website addresses (for full website translations). Additionally, the site offers Tbot—an automated "buddy" that provides translations for Windows Live Messenger. Using the Tbot translator, friends who speak other languages can have one-on-one conversations. Users simply need to add *mtbot@hotmail.com* to their Messenger contacts.

Dictonary.com Translator: *http://translate.reference.com*

This free translator can translate over 50 languages and up to 140 characters at a time. The site also offers a separate Spanish dictionary and translator. At the top of the page, select "Spanish" to view the translator box, as well as the Spanish word of the day, phrase of the day, and grammar tip of the day. The site contains over 750,000 English-Spanish dictionary definitions, example sentences, synonyms, and audio pronunciations.

Google Translate: *http://translate.google.com*

This free translator can translate over 60 languages. Users have the option of copying and pasting text into a box, uploading entire documents, or entering website addresses (for full website translations).

SDL FreeTranslation.com: *http://www.freetranslation.com*

This free translator can translate over 30 languages. Users have the option of copying and pasting text into a box or entering website addresses (for full website translations). The site also offers spoken or emailed translations. A free iPhone application and Facebook translator can also be downloaded.

World Lingo: *http://www.worldlingo.com/en/products_services/worldlingo_translator.html*

This free translator can translate over 30 languages. Users have the option of copying and pasting text into a box, uploading documents, entering website addresses (for website translations), or entering email text (for email translations). Free translations are limited to 500 words.

Yahoo! Babel Fish: *http://babelfish.yahoo.com*

This free translator has a limited language selection; however, the site itself is very user-friendly. Users have the option of copying and pasting up to 150 words into a box or entering website addresses (for full website translations).

When searching online . . .

✪ Add "ELL" and "math" to any search term to narrow the focus.

✪ Search for any strategy, for example "ELL math journals" or "ELL math mnemonics."

✪ Search for math literature using phrases, such as "read about math," "math books for 5th graders," or "math in literature."

✪ Look up the following keywords or phrases:

- ★ teaching strategies
- ★ keywords
- ★ literacy
- ★ graphic organizers
- ★ sentence frames
- ★ assessment
- ★ rubrics

Note: Consider locating specific articles and then cutting and pasting the information into text for student use, as some advertisements may be inappropriate for students.

Bibliography

Anderson, Neil J. "The Role of Metacognition in Second Language Teaching and Learning." Center for Applied Linguistics. April 2002. Accessed January 03, 2012. http://www.cal.org/resources/digest/0110anderson.html.

Barton, Mary Lee, Clare Heidema, and Deborah Jordan. "Teaching Reading in Mathematics and Science." *Educational Leadership* 60, no. 3 (November 2002): 24–28.

Burns, Marilyn. "Marilyn Burns on the Language of Math." *Instructor*, April 2006.

Chamot, Anna Uhl, Kristina Anstrom, Abigail Bartoshesky, Alissa Belanger, Jennifer Delett, Vanessa Karwan, Christine Meloni, Raghad Kadah, and Catharine Keatley. "Language Learning Strategies." In *The Elementary Immersion Learning Strategies Resource Guide*. 2nd ed. Washington, DC: National Capital Language Resource Center. Accessed January 3, 2012. http://www.nclrc.org/eils/.

Dalton, Bridget, and Dana L. Grisham. "eVoc Strategies: 10 Ways to Use Technology to Build Vocabulary." *The Reading Teacher* 64, no. 5 (February 2011): 306–17.

David, Jane L. "Closing the Vocabulary Gap." *Educational Leadership* 67, no. 6 (March 2010): 85–86.

"English Language Learners in Math." Teaching Today. Accessed January 3, 2012. http://teachingtoday.glencoe.com/howtoarticles/english-language-learners-in-math.

"ESOL Strategies—Comprehensible Instruction." UCF College of Education ESOL Education Program. December 4, 2007. Accessed January 3, 2012. http://education.ucf.edu/esol.

Evans, Linda L. "Building Background—Benefits of Using Sentence Frames to Build Background Knowledge." *Ezine @rticles*. Accessed January 3, 2012. http://ezinearticles.com/?Building-Background---Benefits-of-Using-Sentence-Frames-to-Build-Background-Knowledge&id=881703.

Gersten, Russell, Scott K. Baker, and Susan Unok Marks. "What Is Comprehensible Input?" In *Teaching English-Language Learners with Learning Difficulties*, 7–10. Reston, VA: Council Exceptional Children, 1999.

Kennedy, Leonard M., and Steven Tipps. *Guiding Children's Learning of Mathematics*. 8th ed. Albany, NY: Wadsworth Publishing, 1997.

"Lesson 8: Making Inferences." Focused Learning Lessons for Mathematics: Data Analysis, Probability, and Discrete Math. Accessed January 3, 2012. http://www.doe.state.la.us/lde/uploads/5654.pdf.

Macdonald, Heather, and Rebecca Teed. "Interactive Lectures." Starting Point—Teaching Entry Level Geoscience. Accessed January 3, 2012. http://serc.carleton.edu/introgeo/interactive/index.html.

Bibliography *(cont.)*

Ross, Cathy, instr. *How to "Read and Write" in Math: Improving Problem Solving and Communication in Mathematics*. CE Credits Online. Certificate earned April 6, 2011. http://www.cecreditsonline.org.

Simmons, Cindy. Review of *Building Background Knowledge for Academic Achievement*, by Robert J. Marzano. Mississippi Department of Education (September 2007). http://www.mde.k12.ms.us/acad1/text_vacabulary_instruction.DOC

TESOL. *TESOL ESL Standards for Pre-K–12 Students*. Alexandria, VA: TESOL, 1997.

Wetzel, David R. "Math Problem Solving Stories and Case Studies: Using Operational, Logic, and Reasoning Skills in Math." Suite 101. August 28, 2008. Accessed January 3, 2012. http://www.suite101.com/content/math-problem-solving-stories-and-process-skills-a66091.

——. "Teaching Strategies in Math for ESL Students: Instructional Techniques That Increase Comprehension of Concepts." Suite 101. September 23, 2009. Accessed January 3, 2012. http://www.suite101.com/content/teaching-strategies-in-math-for-esl-students-a152018.

Yee, Kevin. "Interactive Techniques." UCF Faculty Center for Teaching & Learning: Selected Pedagogies. Accessed January 3, 2012. http://www.fctl.ucf.edu/TeachingAndLearningResources/SelectedPedagogies/.